Carola Rackete
The Time To Act Is Now

THE TIME TO ACT IS NOW

A call to combat environmental breakdown

Carola Rackete
with Anne Weiss

Translated by Claire Wordley

Cover art: © Céline Keller
Editing: Linguatransfair / Eva Bacon
ISBN: 978-3-755739-67-8

Herstellung und Verlag: BoD – Books on Demand, Norderstedt

**ROSA
LUXEMBURG
STIFTUNG**

Supported by Rosa-Luxemburg-Stiftung with funds of the German foreign office on the
basis of a resolution of the German parliament. The contents of this publication are the sole
responsibilities of the authors and can in no way be taken to reflect the views
of the Rosa-Luxemburg-Stiftung.

To all the victims of civil obedience

Contents

Preface
by Hindou Oumarou Ibrahim
environmental activist from Chad

Where are the men? Sometimes, when you visit a village in the Sahelian bush, you're struck to see communities composed only of women, young boys and old people. Is it a consequence of women's empowerment? Do men stay inside the huts, to prepare the meals? Are they far away from the village, collecting water and wood? Are they the victims of a war or a virus that only targets men between 15 and 50?

No, of course! Men are just away, far, far away. Mostly they are in African cities, living in the slums, trying to find temporary jobs. Some are on desert roads to Libya, some are the slaves of human traffickers, some are helping the human traffickers. A few are on lifeboats on the Mediterranean Sea. And even fewer are in migrant camps at the edge of Europe. They are looking for jobs, they are trying to find a way to send money back to relatives, to feed their families. These men are just looking to regain their pride, their honour. Because in most of these communities, if a man fails to feed his family, he is no longer a man.

We all know the impacts of climate change. They are now visible to every one of us. We watch the forest burning; we watch the ice melting. But we do not realize that one of the most violent impacts of climate change is that it is stealing men and women's dignity.

Since the beginning of this century, in my country, Chad, the average temperature has increased by more than 1.5 °C. It's the same for most African countries. Our trees are burning. Our water reserves are drying up. Our fertile lands are now turning into desert. As an Indigenous woman, I – like others in my community – was used to living and working in harmony with Nature. Seasons, the sun, winds and clouds were our allies. Now they have become our enemy.

Heat waves, with several days of temperatures above 50 °C, kill the men, women, and cattle. Floods destroy the crops. Changes in seasonal rhythms bring new diseases to humans and animals. Lake Chad, which was once among the five largest freshwater reservoirs in Africa, is disappearing before our eyes. When I was born, 30 years ago, it covered 10000 square kilometres. Today, the lake is only 1250 square kilometres. Almost 90 percent has disappeared in my lifetime.

Climate change is like a cancer for the Sahel. It's a disease that dries the lake, but also the hearts of the men and women living there. For centuries, farmers, fishermen and shepherds have lived in harmony. But today, every single drop of fresh water, every single piece of fertile land, is becoming the most precious treasure. People fight for it, and, sometimes, kill for it.

Climate change is a virus that lays the ground for the darkest side of humanity. Groups such as Boko Haram, or other terrorist cells, take advantage of poverty to recruit among the young boys, to encourage communities to fight against each other. In the first months of 2019, European media reported on the massacres of shepherds by farmers, and of farmers by shepherds, in Mali and in Burkina Faso. These people are fighting for the few resources left, encouraged by groups that build an ideology of hate out of extreme poverty.

Why is this happening to us? Why is Mother Earth so hard on us? No one knows, in my community, that the climate is changing because in other parts of the world, the use of fossil fuels is harming the fragile balance of the climate worldwide. As most of the children don't have the chance to go to school, they don't know what is obvious for most of us. Climate change is the consequence of a development model that brings prosperity to a (small) part of this planet, but that is also destroying the livelihood for some of us. The ten last years has been the trailer of a horror movie for the planet and mankind. And my people are the silent witnesses of a problem they did not create.

In the middle of the bush, everywhere in Africa, it is quite easy to find a bottle of Coca-Cola, but almost impossible to find electricity. You will then have to like your soda warm. This is for me the best illustration of the cynicism of our development model. Even in the beginning of the 21st century, in the era of drones, virtual reality and artificial intelligence, half of the African population does not have access to electricity. And electricity is not the only thing missing.

No schools, no decent hospitals, no cures or vaccines for diseases that are considered harmless in the western world.

Climate change is not the only cause of poverty, of course. But climate change is a degenerative disease that obliterates the future of Africa's youth. Where do you find hope when the climate is changing to the point that, when you sow your crops, you have no idea whether it will be a flood or a drought that will annihilate your only source of income?

What can mothers or fathers in the Sahel say to their children when they ask why there's no food on the plate tonight? Is it possible to say, »Don't worry, there is the Paris Agreement, and maybe, if everyone does their part, global warming will stay below 2 °C by the end of the century«? Of course not. So, unless we address the climate crisis, and choose to build a future for this youth, we will not be able to turn the despair into hope. We will not be able to give a solid argument to these communities to prevent them from sending their men to the migration roads.

No one should be forced to leave their home, to risk their life, just because there is no future for them in their native land. No one is happy to leave their family, their roots, their identity. We should never forget that no one is born a migrant. So, we must stand and say clearly that we don't want this future. Then, we have to make changes.

Our time window is short. There is no room either for pessimism or for optimism. Only time for action, and for a fundamental shift in the way we are dealing with the climate problem. No single person has the solution, but every contribution is more than welcome. So, when Carola asked me for a preface for this book, it was obvious for me to say yes. Not only because she is one of many who are actively developing solutions for our world, but also because she is unique in her kind, she believes in global action and sharing responsibility, she risks going to jail to save others' lives. She is a problem solver and one of few people that builds sustainability, equity and justice to ensure a better future for all. Therefore, I encourage you to read her book. I am sure you will be inspired.

Chapter One:
No more hoping

I t's a little before noon and we're still not moving. The stair railing leading up to the ship's bridge is as hot as a radiator pipe. I climb the steps two at a time and when I reach the top I stop for a moment, my skin covered in a thin film of sweat. There is not a whisper of a breeze; the air is still. Really, it's too sweltering to move around; this is the hottest month since climate records began.

Today is Friday, 28 June 2019, and it's been twenty days since we left the Sicilian port of Licata for a rescue mission. We had only been at sea for four days when we rescued 53 people from a fragile raft about 50 nautical miles off the Libyan coast; a raft loaded with men, pregnant women, and minors, including two young children. The Italian Coast Guard has taken the most seriously sick and vulnerable. That leaves forty people on the boat. They're weak and discouraged.

Now we're hoping that someone will tell us what will happen to them.

But we're running out of time.

With every minute that passes, we risk losing another life.

The island of Lampedusa is in sight, sparkling before us like a long, thin band of lights. It's one of the most southern points of Europe and, right now, the nearest safe port. The air is charged with the glittering reflections from the water.

If we were allowed to, we could reach the harbour in an hour. Instead, we're stuck here, waiting for the European states to find a solution. I look across the deck, where the speedboats are stowed, and the main deck below. To shield the lower decks against the sun we've hung up tarps; under them lie all the people we've saved from the raft.

We can't care for so many people on this ship for very long. She only has three bathrooms, and while we can purify seawater for drinking, the process takes ages. Even with the tank we refilled at the port, there's not enough water for this many people to wash and do their laundry regularly. What is more, those sleeping on the boat deck have to make do with just one blanket. It's not comfortable there; either you fold the blanket as a mattress and freeze all night, or you wrap yourself in it to keep warm but before long every part of your body touching the PVC-tiled floor will be aching.

All around us the sea sparkles and the small waves break against the hull of the boat. *Sea-Watch 3* is an old offshore supply vessel from the seventies, once used by the oil industry before falling into the hands of Médecins Sans Frontières before she was finally acquired by Sea-Watch using donations from their supporters. In short, a big ship that requires a lot of maintenance.

She does the job, of course, but I don't like her very much.

The truth is that, under different circumstances, I wouldn't be here. This year, I wasn't planning to embark on any »missions,« the Sea-Watch term for rescue operations. Not that I haven't spent some years at sea, mainly as navigating officer on board large research vessels in the Arctic, and also with Greenpeace; but then I did a master's degree in environmental conservation and, when I finished, I wanted to concentrate on protecting the natural world.

To be honest, I've never been a seafaring enthusiast, and after dedicating a few years to my profession, I felt it was more important to fight for the preservation of our biosphere. But my nautical knowledge came in handy when I started collaborating with Sea-Watch and other rescue NGOs doing something that I consider essential: saving lives.

A few short weeks ago I received an email telling me that the captain of a rescue mission due to start in the next few days had fallen ill. At the time, I was busy in Scotland, where I was working as a trainee on a conservation programme. What we were doing, basically, was collecting data on butterflies, maintaining the hiking trails, and most recently, when torrential rains fell, spending three days in the greenhouse transplanting Scots pines.

The landscape in that part of Scotland is beautiful: steep-sloped mountains cloaked with dark, mossy hoods, where the smell of wet meadows combines with conifer resin and the fragrance of delicate flowers. At night you can hear the squawking of the little loons over the fog-wrapped sea. The air is so clear, so full of aromas, that if I could, I would have spent every hour of the day outside.

In short, I didn't want to leave. But that message was sent to everyone on the emergency contact list – a list of everyone who could replace a crew member at the last minute. Whereas volunteers for unskilled jobs are easy to recruit, it's much more difficult to find people qualified to handle a ship or provide medical care.

My intuition told me that Sea-Watch would struggle to

find a replacement in such a short time, and when I spoke to the head of operations on the phone, he confessed that he had no one who could captain the boat. If I didn't do it, the ship couldn't sail, even though she had all the other necessary crew. Feeling the weight of responsibility, I packed my bags.

That's why I'm here now, in the middle of this scorching summer, on a boat anchored in southern Europe. Above the splash of the waves I hear a few snippets of conversation from time to time; otherwise, all is calm. I've gone over everything we can do, both with the crew and with the Sea-Watch team on land, where we have lots of volunteers and a handful of employees working mainly from Berlin, but also Amsterdam, Rome, Brussels, and other cities. This is the team that deals with logistics, media, and internal communications, in addition to providing legal advice and political advocacy work. They are in contact with other organisations and political actors on land, and provide the crew with information and advice on what's going on.

We've been trapped in international waters for two weeks now. Via our unreliable internet connection, I've sent out an email to the competent bodies in Rome and Valletta asking for their support, and also the Den Helder coastguard headquarters, because *Sea-Watch 3* is flying the Dutch flag. Via the German Ministry of Foreign Affairs, we've also asked Spain and France for assistance.

Several members of the Italian Coast Guard boarded the ship. Then came the Guardia di Finanza, the customs and tax police that reports to the Italian Ministry of Economy and Finance in Rome. They told us to wait. They said they had no solutions for us.

Nothing happened.

We were running out of possibilities. It became increasingly difficult to keep people safe on our ship; the people we rescued were in urgent need of medical attention. One of the women confessed to our doctor that she was so desperate, she was contemplating suicide. She told her that she felt safer with someone by her side.

But we can't give her what she needs. Our crew consists of more than twenty people, including engineers and maritime-technical personnel such as myself, but also medical specialists and the speedboat crew. Most of them are volunteers, such as Oscar, a student about to graduate from law school. There are only three people employed by Sea-Watch, but some volunteers have been involved for a long time – like Lorenz, who takes care of our passengers. Staff or volunteer, everyone is assigned their shifts, in order to ensure we can care for people day and night. But with mounting uncertainty and their already precarious condition worsening, this is becoming increasingly difficult.

So, two days ago, I declared a state of emergency and entered Italian waters without proper authorisation. The Guardia di Finanza stopped us, took the crew's details and checked the ship's documentation. They said a political solution to our situation would soon be found, and in the meantime we would just have to wait.

And, having said that, they left again.

Yesterday, in view of our plight, I asked once again to be allowed to dock in the port. And, again, we were stopped by vessels from the Italian authorities.

»The solution is imminent,« they said.

Then a chartered boat arrived with journalists and a few MPs on board.

Lots of cameras.

Lots of phone calls.

And no solutions.

Today we received a message from the Italian Public Prosecutor's Office informing us that an investigation has been opened against me for promoting illegal immigration. Although it may sound strange, this is our first ray of hope in a long time. On our last mission in May, an investigation launched by the Public Prosecutor's Office led to the vessel being seized. If such an order were given now, the Prosecutor's Office would have to take responsibility for the people on board, and they would finally be able to disembark.

That is exactly what we are waiting for today.

I raise a hand to my forehead, shading my eyes and wiping away the sweat. Around us there are fishing boats coming and going, and a few yachts leaving the harbour. If we weren't going through this terrible situation, we'd be taking a dip right now. But for now we have to stay on the ship, roasting in the heat.

According to what I am told later, 17 boats have arrived in Lampedusa in recent days, carrying 300 people. That is, 300 refugees, mostly from Tunisia, who have managed against the odds to reach the Italian coast. The perilous vessels they travel in are called *ghost boats*. As the people on them are already in territorial waters, the Coast Guard simply lets them approach land and then notifies the police or the humanitarian services. Usually, the passengers do not try to flee or hide, because Lampedusa is so small as to make hiding futile. Normally a fisherman or some other resident spots the refugees before their rickety boat reaches the beach or the cliffs. Then the authorities come to take them to the reception centre, where they are identified and fingerprinted.

Only we are still being held here, with forty refugees in urgent need of medical care. There are people with physical ailments that require immediate attention, such as those whose illnesses have worsened on board and who we can no longer treat effectively because they have high fever or severe pain. It was these, the sickest people, who were taken by the Coast Guard. A majority of the passengers are suffering from post-traumatic stress disorder. There are others with older injuries documenting the violence they were exposed to in the Libyan camps, or with broken bones, who should be treated immediately. According to the Italian Coast Guard, these ailing people are not in a state of emergency. In this way, a question of maritime law has been turned into an absurd discussion about the health status of the refugees who, like all people, healthy or otherwise, have a right to a safe harbour.

In our morning meeting, Lorenz, a qualified nurse who, as passenger coordinator, is in charge of looking after our passengers, once again sums up the difficult situation: »The biggest danger,« he says, »is that people will decide to act on their own. I'm afraid they might jump overboard.« Lorenz is a thin, brown-haired man with one side of his head shaved. He's been going on missions as long as I have and also studied environmental science. That's one thing we have in common, in addition to the fact that we're both here for the same reason. No one signs up for something like this for the sake of adventure, or on some insubstantial whim.

No member of the crew would. Nor would I, or the people we rescue.

Quite the contrary, these refugees are all fleeing violence. Most of them have made their worst experiences on the last leg of their journey, in Libya, a country torn apart by civil war.

Lorenz tells me that when talking with them about the conditions in the Libyan camps, one might say: »See this head wound? That came from a metal pipe.« On someone else he sees ten cigarette burns on their body. One man lifts up his shirt and shows Lorenz a scar. »These were electric shocks,« he tells him.

»These people don't mind showing their wounds because they've become normal to them. Almost all of them have been tortured,« Lorenz says.

He wants to help make the world a better place, one shaped more by freedom than discrimination. He is one of the volunteers who has been on countless Sea-Watch missions, and for this he sacrifices a lot, above all a regular life. Again and again, he repeats what each of us is thinking: how incredibly strong – and kind – these people are, despite all they've been through. And how alive they are, given everything they have seen and suffered.

According to medical reports, many of our passengers are suffering from the violence and torment inflicted on them in the Libyan camps: fractured bones, bayonet blows, and burns from hot plastic poured on their skin, not to mention, of course, post-traumatic stress disorder. On their heads they have visible scars and, on their souls, invisible ones, from the beatings, threats, trafficking, and enslavement they have suffered, from the fear of death and, among the women, from the rape and prostitution to which they have been forced by threats to their families. Many are dehydrated from seasickness, which further aggravates their condition. As a result, they suffer from sleep disorders, nervousness, anxiety, and lack of impulse control.

»All these injuries reflect the reports of what is happening in the refugee camps and along the migrant routes,« Victoria, the doctor responsible for the medical reports, points out. She specialises in anaesthesiology and emergency medicine, and has worked for years in the intensive care unit of a Hamburg hospital. This is the first time she's been involved in a rescue operation, and also the first time she has spent so much time away from her children. »It makes me incredibly angry that the world is so unfair, so I felt I had to do something.«

The Coast Guard initially took ten refugees whose lives were in immediate danger, but had to come back twice more to deal with further emergencies. One man lost consciousness; another suffered severe abdominal pain and was evacuated along with his brother, who is still a minor. Every time one of the refugees was taken away, the others formed a double line to let the sick person past: they wanted to say goodbye to them, even to the unconscious. I was touched to see such connection between people who had never met before and were forced to live together in crowded conditions.

Other than collecting the most seriously ill passengers, the men of the Coast Guard don't do much. They understand our situation – they know very well what it's like, as they used to do sea rescue off the coast of Libya. They're quite nice but completely useless for the time being, because they're only helping us as much as they're allowed to. Every time they evacuate a refugee, the others ask us if they have to fall as seriously ill before they can leave the ship too.

These people need to reach a safe harbour and go ashore – now. I cannot imagine how difficult the wait is for someone who's been through what they have. The departure into the unknown, the long journey across the desert, hunger, deprivation, false promises, assaults. The utter despair of being held indefinitely in an internment camp, torture, rape, seeing your friends and family shot. The fear of dying in a fragile inflatable raft in the middle of the sea.

The Mediterranean is much more dangerous than most vacationers imagine; the weather can change in the blink of an eye, which means that a raft with four air chambers doesn't offer much in the way of protection. If just one of these chambers loses air, the boat, already heavily overloaded, can sink.

»I have great respect for the sea,« says Oscar. He's a law student, and by driving our speedboats, he risks not being admitted to the bar association if he ends up tried and convicted for taking part in these missions. The Mediterranean is a huge sea, and it's easy to get lost in her waters. On *Sea-Watch 3* we have technical equipment that can save our lives in an emergency. From the speedboat, all we can see are the wind-churned waves, but suddenly, we come across a dinghy full of people barely a metre above the water. Hardly any of the occupants can swim; in rough seas they're in great danger, because the floor of the dinghy or one of the air chambers could break. Then the rescue operation becomes more complicated, because, naturally, panic sets in. The petrol drums on board are often uncapped, and when the boat capsizes, the petrol spills into the sea along with the people. Anyone swallowing as much as a mouthful of this toxic mix will faint and drown. On inflatable boats, people sit right on the edges, with pregnant women and small children in the middle. Every time I see that, I realise what a risk these people are taking. How much misery must a person have suffered to go through such danger? As soon as they're on the beach and the boat is ready for the last leg of their journey, they're left with no choice. Some of them are even forced to get on. And still there are politicians insisting that these boats are perfectly seaworthy, or that people are making the crossing voluntarily … They're so incredibly cynical, they should come out with us and have the experience first-hand.

What must it be like to sit there, in a cheap, overloaded dinghy, completely exposed to the forces of nature, while the wooden planks precariously attached to the floor bang against the air chambers until they break? How would you feel to be sitting in such a boat, sailing without a crew, without a life jacket, without drinking water, even without enough fuel for the next day? What thoughts cross your mind when you can't swim and the boat takes on water and starts to sink?

Nobody would get into such a boat if they thought they were going to die on the crossing. But this is no small danger, far from it, as there are hardly any ships left out there that can come to their rescue. The EU naval missions, the Italian Coast Guard and the European Border and Coast Guard Agency (Frontex) have disappeared from the waters. The private rescue missions are the only ones here, and we can't be everywhere at the same time, not least because the

European authorities are making our work ever more difficult.

We don't know how many shipwrecks there have been in the central Mediterranean off the Libyan coast in recent years. The official figures only count the bodies pulled from the sea, or washed up on the beaches of Libya and Tunisia. The actual number of casualties, of those who sink forever and are not pulled out from the waves or washed ashore, is much higher. According to the United Nations Refugee Agency (UNHCR), more than 18,000 people have died or gone missing in the Mediterranean since 2014. My crew, too, has been on missions where they ended up finding only bodies floating on the water.

What scares the refugees most is that they might be forced to return to Libya, where they were last locked up. Many rescue reports write of people jumping off boats to their deaths upon seeing the Libyan Coast Guard about to collect them; they have a visceral fear that the Libyans will recapture them and put them in a camp again. According to a leaked telegram from the German embassy in Niger, diplomats who have been on site in Libyan camps reported »concentration-camp like conditions«, where »gross human rights violations are systematically practised«. The traumatic memories from these camps haunt our passengers in the days and, above all, the nights they spend on our ship. They stew in their memories as much as they do in this heat. Still, they're being forced to stay on board our ship for so long that their situation keeps getting worse and worse. Our governments wouldn't leave a European exposed to these conditions. If these people held German, French, or Italian passports, they would have been back on dry land days ago. They would be on talk shows and the hosts would ask them how they felt, and which politician or authority they thought had failed to act. They would give interviews to the mainstream magazines and maybe even write a book. The public would be enraged, finding it utterly intolerable to see people suffer such trauma while fleeing their countries or being detained in refugee camps.

But our passengers obviously don't have the right skin colour. They happened to be born in other countries. That's why people assume that it's nothing to them to be crammed into a crowded boat and endure this sticky heat. Because they were not born in a rich country. Because they don't have the right passport. Nobody wants anything to do with them.

Only if a person's life is seriously at risk do we have the right to enter a port – even in a country like Italy that has closed its ports to vessels like ours.

On day sixteen I am once again on the verge of making use of that right. As I was on the two previous days, when the authorities kept delaying us with assurances that the European states were close to finding a solution to our problem.

For now, we're still hoping they'll let us enter the port.

In the meantime, our voyage has made international headlines. The world looks at the ship waiting in the waters of Lampedusa with more attention than it has paid to any of the many rescue operations previously undertaken by private vessels. This scrutiny is partly because of the current political situation; the Italian Interior Minister has passed a new decree with the support of his party, a right-wing nationalist league, banning civilian rescue vessels from Italy's territorial waters. This puts us in a difficult situation as a maritime rescue service, because all those who contravene the new rule are accused of encouraging illegal immigration and are subject to heavy fines. If the world is suddenly so interested in the rescue operations, it is also because of the minister himself, who keeps tweeting about it, and because the rescue ship is captained by a young woman – me.

It's not because of the actual scandal.

It's not because these people are trapped here, or that they're being treated as second-class human beings.

This is simply racism.

The appropriateness of sea rescue is often presented as a matter of opinion. This is total nonsense.

According to Article 98 of the United Nations Convention on the Law of the Sea (UNCLOS), a ship's captain is obliged to render assistance to shipwrecked persons if he or she can reasonably be expected to do so.

It is generally accepted that »distress at sea« occurs when there is a serious risk that the crew and passengers of a boat could lose their lives, irrespective of the cause of distress.

Rescuing people in distress at sea is mandatory under international law, and sea rescue is regulated in many conventions relating to the Law of the Sea. According to UNCLOS, for example, states are obliged to organise and maintain an adequate rescue service. We rescued the shipwrecked people in international waters, in Libya's search and rescue zone, which extends 70 nautical miles from the Libyan coast. Because there is no safe harbour in Libya and the state under whose flag the *Sea-Watch 3* is sailing has failed to provide us with instructions, we set course for Lampedusa. The Italian island is the nearest safe harbour, which is why its authorities ought to take in the people we've rescued. Malta's search and rescue zone extends around Italy's territorial waters, so we also asked Malta to grant us access to a safe harbour – but they refused on the spot.

Of course we verify that the refugees are in distress before we take them on board. But the condition of these boats can almost always be counted as »distress at sea«: they're not seaworthy, which in itself poses an imminent danger to their occupants, and on top of that, the vessels hardly ever carry life jackets, water reserves, or navigation equipment. The people in these dinghies are in grave danger, which is why we take them aboard.

It is often said that if refugees try to cross the sea, then organisations like ours are to blame, because we come to their rescue, thus creating what is called a »pull factor«. The Italian Coast Guard was reproached with the same argument when they first took up rescue operations. NGOs only started saving people at sea after tens of thousands of people had drowned in the Mediterranean. A study has now revealed what percentage of refugee boats are leaving the Libyan coast at any given time compared to the number of rescue ships sailing in the area. The statistics show that the increase in refugee boats bears no relation to the number of rescue vessels present in those waters. But what is also clear is that the fewer rescue vessels there are, the higher the number of deaths. Even if there is only one rescue vessel, even if there are none, the refugee boats still go out.

Many people resent the fact that we're taking refugees to Europe instead of sending them to Tunisia or Libya, but the definition of »safe harbour« shouldn't vary with a person's passport or country of origin. Moreover, we can't take rescued people to Libya, because returning a person to a state where they face torture and death is in contravention of international law. They have no protection in Tunisia either. Tunisia does not have an asylum system that guarantees the safety of people persecuted because of their sexual orientation or political opinions. In fact, official European ships never take people to Libya or Tunisia. Moreover, Tunisia won't allow us to enter its territorial waters, not even to refuel. They don't want to become Europe's offloading port. Ideally we'd want to hand the refugees over to the European authorities right here and right now, so their ships can take them to a safe harbour and we can go back to saving lives. But as the safe harbours remain closed to us, and as we are forced to wait for the authorities to find a definitive solution to our problem, time is taking its toll on the lives of many people.

Both in parliaments and on television, there are debates about who should save refugees at sea, and for what reasons. Meanwhile, the death toll is rising. According to the International Organisation for Migration (IOM), the southern Mediterranean is the most dangerous border in the world for refugees and migrants. Instead of helping them, the only thing that's being done on the safe side of the border is discussing the validity of the different reasons why a person might leave their home. As if we, as industrialised countries, were not in part responsible for their plight.

We are asking the wrong questions. Sea rescue missions don't distinguish who they save.

What matters is saving people at risk of drowning. The

German writer Heinrich Böll supported the *Cap Anamur*, whose crew saved countless Vietnamese boat people in the early 1980s. He refused to accept any compromise when it came to moral responsibility: »It seems to me that we must save lives wherever we can. No institution that has the capacity to save human lives can make a selection on the high seas from among those who are there. Because that would be arbitrarily condemning people to death,« the Nobel laureate told the German weekly *Der Spiegel* in 1981.

For me, too, it is beyond doubt that we must rescue refugees and migrants. The question that needs to be asked is: why are they getting into these unstable boats to get to Europe in the first place? And because people don't want them here, we need to fight the causes of migration, as governments like to say. But for that, they would have to change a system from which they themselves are benefiting.

A system whose power structures have been in place since the colonial era.

A system that is essentially incompatible with our values.

In their quest for continued prosperity and growth, industrialised nations have always taken advantage of the countries and the people in the poorer parts of our planet. In colonial times those people were deprived of their political, economic, and cultural independence; the most visible sign of this is arbitrary border demarcations, which are still a source of conflict today. Economic hegemony continues today through monoculture systems that degrade the soil and require the use of pesticides and artificial fertilisers. As a result, steppes are spreading and deserts are forming, to the detriment of soil quality and biodiversity. Forests are being lost and Indigenous people are being driven off their lands. Often these monocultures occupy land where staple foods – urgently needed by the local population – should be grown. Countries that turn to growing only a handful of crops are incredibly dependent on the international market. In the case of cocoa and coffee, prices are often imposed by speculators; they are export commodities that are highly prone to crises.

Colonial-era power structures continue to shape many countries in the Global South today. With their economies geared towards exporting raw materials and their markets flooded with cheap products from industrialised countries, they continue to surrender to the richer Global North. They are forced to sign free trade agreements prohibiting import tariffs, preventing them from protecting their own industries. These countries are the dumping grounds for our trash. On top of that, their debts often force them to sell access rights to their fisheries, exposing their marine resources to destruction before their very eyes.

If we want to speak about refugees coming over to Europe in boats, the first thing we need to talk about is global inequality. The prosperity of a few countries, large multinational corporations, and wealthy individuals is based on the exploitation of the labour and mineral resources of poor countries. Industrialised countries on the European continent and in other parts of the world bear a significant responsibility for the civil wars, economic hardship, exploitation, mistreatment, and abuse that others suffer; indeed, they profit from it all. We live in a globalised world and we, in European countries, are among the few who benefit.

Our electronic waste is exported to Ghana; our T-shirts are manufactured in low-wage countries like Bangladesh;

the raw materials for our mobile phones come from Congo, where children mine cobalt and coltan in inhumane conditions. Our way of life directly impacts the existence of people in the Global South, bringing in its wake diseases, pollution, and work without social security. Our hunger for energy and the emissions it causes are fuelling the climate crisis, which hits hardest those countries that have contributed the least to heating our planet. This in turn exacerbates poverty around the globe – and the causes that force people to flee their countries.

As long as our economic system continues to generate social inequalities this extreme, as long as nature continues to be exploited throughout the world, there will always be people risking their lives in boats that no one would willingly board. That's why this is not a »refugee crisis«.

It's a global justice crisis.

And it's threatening to undermine our European values.

The values on which the community of European states is built can be found in various declarations – from international human rights treaties and the Charter of Fundamental Rights of the European Union to the German constitution itself – all so well formulated that I would subscribe to every word. But unfortunately, they're not worth the paper they're written on, as our current *Sea-Watch 3* mission is proving. We've been kept at sea for two weeks now. The way we're being treated stands in stark contrast to all the values the EU claims to embody. It's harsh response is triggered by an economic rationale, which only goes to prove that this is an economic community struggling to uphold its values.

The writer Ilija Trojanow recently published an »Open Letter to Europe« in which he portrayed the European Union as an incarnation of Dr Jekyll and Mr Hyde. Taking on the role of Dr Jekyll, we see European politicians launch into passionate speeches in defence of human rights and against the destruction of nature. But »whenever money is involved or ›our‹ prosperity under threat,« Trojanow notes, »Mr Hyde rears his ugly head and sabotages the struggle for human dignity and a decent life for all.«

Even solidarity among European states is eroding – due to economic squabbles.

The Dublin III regulation, which requires asylum seekers to apply for asylum in the European country through which they entered the continent, shifts all obligations to the states in southern Europe. Countries such as Italy, Malta, and Greece are left to shoulder the responsibility for refugees on their own because the EU does nothing. Italy and Malta have already experienced some European states agreeing to accept a certain number of refugees but then waiting weeks, even months before actually taking them in.

Italy launched its rescue operation, called Mare Nostrum, a few days after a rusty barge carrying 545 refugees from Eritrea and Somalia caught fire very close to the anchorage where we are now. The incident, which occurred on 3 October 2013, killed 366 people. The military divers who recovered the bodies from the sea were severely traumatised. There were so many bodies that body bags had to be placed along the Lampedusa harbour, a horrifying sight which sent shockwaves across the island and the entire country.

The Mare Nostrum operation had a monthly cost of around nine million euros, and because of Dublin III the other European states left Italy with the sole responsibility to deal with both the cost and the refugees. This led to the operation being increasingly scaled down, until it was completely suspended in 2014. Because there were no longer any state rescue vessels operating in the Mediterranean, Sea-Watch sent their first private rescue vessel from Germany in 2015. The aim was to observe the situation and draw Europe's attention to the refugees making the crossing, so that the EU would once again coordinate rescue operations to be undertaken by state bodies. Sea-Watch called for safe passage for migrants to ensure that the Mediterranean would not become a mass grave.

Unfortunately, these demands have not been heard. Indeed, without NGOs like Sea-Watch, there wouldn't be any sea rescue missions in the Mediterranean at all. We are effectively taking on the work that states are refusing to do because it jeopardises their economic system.

If there are no safe harbours in Libya, it is partly because Europe has played a not so insignificant role in its civil war – again for economic reasons. Libya has the largest oil reserves on the African continent, as well as large deposits of natural gas, and this obviously arouses tremendous greed – so much greed that some people are willing to sacrifice the lives of others to get their hands on these fuels. The Libyan population, and refugees from other African countries, have been caught between the fronts of a war that began several years ago.

The situation in Libya is now somewhat confused due to shifting alliances and the obscure objectives of the actors involved. But it's clear that France, Italy, and other Western European countries are getting involved in the conflict and supporting the rebels, since major European companies, such as the Italian oil company ENI, France's global player Total, and Germany's Wintershall (BASF), are extracting raw materials in Libya. The situation is further complicated by the fact that Marshal Khalifa Hafter, head of the rebel military forces, controls most of Libya's oil reserves, while the government of Fayez al Sarraj, recognised by the international community, is using its anti-migration deal to put Europe under pressure – a deal based on conditions that are inhumane: According to the agreement, EU member states no longer send military vessels to save refugees shipwrecked in the Mediterranean; they are only observed from the sky. In Libya, the European Union is funding a coastguard service that is staffed by militia members and sends those it »rescues« back to a country at civil war, where they face gross and systematic human rights violations: torture, indefinite detention, sexual abuse. While the EUNAVFOR MED operation is withdrawing ships from migrant crossing areas, Frontex is fine-tuning its surveillance systems in the Mediterranean. More than 100 million euros are being spent on monitoring using satellites and unmanned drones – possibly making the Mediterranean one of the most-surveilled maritime areas in the world. The »moat« of Fortress Europe has become a testing ground for innovative technologies to combat migration at the expense of the refugees themselves, and there has been no public outcry.

All this serves to put up walls rather than save human lives. The death rate among those who dare to cross the Mediterranean has risen sharply. We, with our rescue operation, are making it very clear that there is no question about whether someone should be saved or not.

Like any captain, I have an obligation to rescue anyone

in distress. No matter whether they are sailors or refugees, no matter where they come from or where they want to go. No seafarer has the slightest doubt in this matter. Providing assistance to shipwrecked boats and ships is not only a fundamental obligation of every person at sea, but also an expression of humanity. If I go to prison for saving people from the Mediterranean, I'll do so with a clear conscience. Because what I have done isn't wrong – but instead, the only right thing in an inhumane system.

Ultimately I'm defending values that we all share, values that seem to be fading as Europe is putting up more and more walls around its borders.

We're facing a simple question here: do we want to leave the people seeking our help out to die, or do we want to save them?

But members of my generation, those who will inhabit this planet for some time to come, are also asking a larger question: how do we want to treat those fleeing their country in the future – and how do we want them to treat us?

It seems to me that, in these changing times, it is important to talk about how we envision our future as a society. Today, even states that are traditionally considered to be immigrant nations, whose founding fathers were migrants, are combating people's movements in the most inhumane ways. Think of the United States closing the Mexican border to »illegal« immigrants. Think also of Australia, imposing its own »Pacific Solution« by locking migrants up in detention centres on the islands of Manus and Nauru to keep them from applying for asylum on the Australian mainland. This form of false imprisonment is accompanied by poor medical care and abysmal hygiene conditions, as well as rape and assault of inmates. People living in confinement are denied privacy and dignified living conditions, resulting in self-harm, suicide attempts, and deaths.

Until recently, flight or expulsion from one's homeland was a plight faced by many Europeans. We need only go back a few decades to the time of our grandparents and great-grandparents, many of whom in my country were refugees from the East, from the territories that Germany lost in World War II. Going back even further, there are the millions who emigrated to the United States in the 19th century, forced to abandon their homes by a great famine that killed a million people in Ireland and caused a million more to leave their country and seek their fortunes overseas. People have fled wars and persecution because they were Jewish, or because they were political dissidents, or because they risked becoming victims of ethnic cleansing. Today, the people fleeing their homes are coming to Europe, to this island of prosperity that closes its borders as if to an enemy. But today we are at the beginning of much larger migration movements – and driven by completely different causes.

According to the scientific consensus and due to the continuing increase in emissions worldwide, our planet's climate will continue to heat up. This will lead to crippled harvests and severe water shortages, all of which will result in ever more social conflicts. Lack of food and conflict typically force many people to leave their homes, usually for other parts of the same country, as most do not have the financial means to go any further. Only a small fraction make it across international borders. If the climate crisis progresses, more and more people will have to seek out new places to live. What we have seen in the Mediterranean is just a taste of what millions of people will have to face in the future.

We are perhaps the last generation that can still avoid this fate. To do so, we must halt the over-consumption of resources and address global injustices and the violation of human rights. We can no longer wait for someone to do something, for states to take responsibility, for another climate summit ending in a lot of talk and no resolutions.

Our situation aboard the *Sea-Watch 3* mirrors these global challenges. The time has come to act, because we have to get the people on board to safety. Sixteen days have passed since their rescue, so I no longer believe that politicians and the relevant authorities have a sense of responsibility. Governments, it seems, are incapable of finding a joint solution. There are several German cities that are willing to take in our refugees. German Interior Minister Horst Seehofer wanted the rescue to be registered on Italian territory, under the Dublin III regulation, but Italy has refused to do so. Yesterday, several MEPs came to our boat and assured us that something would be done soon.

We took their word for it, so we moved slowly through the waters and then dropped anchor.

We are trapped because we trusted them.

Because we trusted the Guardia di Finanza and the Coast Guard, European laws and decrees, the UN Refugee Convention, governments, and ministers.

Nothing is happening.

Even the European Court of Human Rights, which we asked for protection when we were looking for a safe harbour, has ruled that Italy is not responsible for the refugees because our ship was outside its territorial waters when we picked them up; according to the high court, the refugees were no longer in danger.

While we're sweating buckets on the boat, important people comfortably ensconced in their air-conditioned offices have decided to do nothing. Soon, we may need another emergency transport like the one yesterday that took the seriously ill refugee and his brother.

My team and I are worried that the mood will shift. Most of the refugees are desperate; last night was a horror show because another sick person had to be moved urgently. Even though we're exhausted, at the end of our strength, we keep twice as many staff on watch as before – even with the MEPs on board – so that we're able to intervene in time in case someone tries to do something desperate.

In case someone tries to commit suicide.

In case someone jumps into the water to try to swim ashore.

Which more or less amounts to the same thing given the exhausted state the refugees are in. Our medical team and our passenger coordinator, Lorenz, are very worried.

It's too late now to head for another harbour.

Should I wait until another emergency happens?

Risk someone dying?

The day stretches like chewing gum in the sun. The atmosphere is tense. In the afternoon, the Italian Guardia di Finanza and the Italian Coast Guard come and spend hours collecting evidence about our alleged collaboration in illegal immigration. They make copies of the photos and videos of the rescue and all our emails. When they leave the boat five hours later, they tell me again that I must stand by.

I still have hope. At the end of the afternoon we receive the news that the Italian prosecutor's office will not confiscate our boat, even though they've opened an investigation, so the refugees are still my responsibility. It is quite clear: waiting has not helped me, or the refugees. We're in the same position as ten days ago, but with the additional complication that the refugees are now in a worse state.

I have to consider my options: should I ignore the embargo and just head for port?

I think back to what Lorenz and Victoria have told me about our passengers' condition. It's far more important to me to ensure these people are safe than that we keep our boat, *Sea-Watch 3*, from being confiscated by the authorities. Personal consequences rank third. I don't care if I'm arrested. The situation is too critical.

The decision I am making is not an impulsive one, as some of the people who will later see this on the news may believe. I've weighed our options carefully, but it's clear that we have exhausted all possibilities, politically and legally. In the short term, no one is going to help us. A little while ago we received a communiqué from the German Foreign Ministry informing us that Italy is still blocking a political solution. We have our backs to the wall.

I call the crew to announce my decision, a decision that from my point of view is inevitable. When we meet on the bridge it's eleven p. m.

»I don't want to risk another night,« I tell them. »We've reached a point where we don't know how the people will react, or if any of them will jump overboard in the middle of the night. Despite the many promises we've been given, we have no guarantee that we'll be allowed to disembark any time soon. Quite the opposite, because the talks between Italy and the other EU states are once again at an impasse.« Everyone knows that we have crossed two red lines that we set ourselves at the beginning of our mission. One is the danger of suicide, and the other is the loss of control over what happens on deck. »So I've decided to set course for the port.«

I do what needs to be done because others chose to do nothing.

No more hoping. It's time to act.

Chapter Two:
A humanitarian imperative

As I look at the map of the harbour, I hear voices outside the bridge. On deck, they're getting ready to dock. It takes a long time before I hear the anchor windlass starting.

We're ready. I radio the port, but they don't answer as there's nobody on duty at night. I order the crew to hoist the anchor – and we're on our way. High time, as it is already past midnight. A few minutes later, Dan, our boatswain, tells me that the anchor has become entangled in an old fishing net. It takes a little over half an hour until we're finally free.

I'm about to set off again when Sören, the chief engineer, comes to the bridge. He is dressed in his usual overalls, a black cap with coloured buttons covering his dark blonde Mohawk and wide sideburns.

»The bow thruster isn't working,« he says. »But we'll fix it right away.« And with that he heads back to the engine room.

That's the last thing we needed. It's Murphy's Law; today everything that can go wrong, does goes wrong.

The bow thruster is a propulsion mechanism below the waterline that makes it easier to manoeuvre in the port. Fixing it will delay our departure, and who knows what else might happen. But then, ten minutes later, the phone rings: we're finally ready to go.

Before meeting the crew, I downed a coffee; I haven't

been sleeping well for the last few nights, constantly being woken up to deal with some new important issue.

Now I'm calm, focused. I've tried to convey to the crew that the entry into port is purely routine. I can only imagine what's going on down there, on the deck where our passengers are lying, or what they're thinking. We had to move them to the dinghy deck because we need the main deck for docking.

At midnight, Lorenz and the rest of the crew gathered the people together. »The moment we've been waiting for has arrived. We're heading for the harbour, so pack your things.«

Lorenz later tells me that the response was oddly subdued, despite the good news. »I thought it was going to be a moment of joy, that everyone would cheer when they heard the news. Some did seem happy, but overall there was sadness and despondency. We didn't have the time to discuss this, but I'm convinced that if they reacted this way, it was because of the uncertainty they felt about leaving a safe place and not knowing what awaits them in Europe.«

We're getting closer and closer to the port of Lampedusa. The streetlamps reflect in the dark waters of the inner harbour.

It's cool on the bridge because the air conditioning is on – it's one of the few places on the ship that's equipped with one. It's as dark in here as it is outside, the only lights the red and green ones on the navigation panel. Due to the day's heat, I'm still wearing a black tank top and have tied my dreadlocks up in a bun. The customs police boat cruises in front of us to block us from entering the harbour. I hear the radio crackling as they tell me again and again that I don't have permission to enter the port. We move forward slowly, but stay our course.

There's only one berth in the small harbour where *Sea-Watch 3* can moor, so that's where we have to go.

Because the island is so small, the harbour is right in the airport's approach path. When the ferry or ships of our size want to dock, the airport has to be closed. For this reason I said days ago that if necessary we would sail in at night, when there's no air traffic anyway.

As I'm about to dock the ship, the customs police dart between us and the pier. I later learn that the Italian Ministry of the Interior had ordered them to block our passage.

I move the boat to sail behind the police. They also move back, blocking us again.

I step out onto the balcony of the bridge wing to get a better look at them. Our boat is now alongside the quay, almost at a standstill, but between us and the pier are the police. For a moment it seems as if time has stopped.

After a while they finally take their lines. I see the trail of water behind them: they're leaving.

I draw a deep breath and return to the bridge to continue docking. Just then I hear voices on the radio: they tell me we've hit the patrol.

I leap out to see for myself. Sure enough, the customs boat is stuck between *Sea-Watch 3*, the pier and a large black fender, but then manages to pass us and settles directly behind us on the pier.

I don't like the fact that our boats have touched, but right now I have to concentrate on docking. So I return to the bridge and steer the boat towards the quay. Several members of our crew throw out the mooring lines to people waiting on shore. Some of them I know because they're crew members of a rescue plane that I was on last year; others are sympathetic Lampedusans. I even recognize the village priest. We've made it.

At last.

I know that now the next act begins.

When I get back on the deck I hear shouts from the harbour. So many people are gathered, right there on the quayside.

Some are carrying banners and applauding us, including some of my friends.

There are television cameras and commentators, there are journalists and photographers causing a storm of lights and flashes.

There's also a small group of citizens, some shouting at the top of their voices. »Shame on you,« yells a man, while next to him a woman raises her fist and shrieks, her face contorted: »You're a trafficker! You should be arrested!«

And then there is the long line of policemen with their arms folded.

The whole drama of Europe's refugee policy is being played out on a stage of fifty square metres. At first nothing happens, as the police don't allow us to get a gangway in place and disembark. But an hour later we have several customs officers on the boat.

»You're under arrest,« one of them tells me. Shortly after, they lead me off the boat to where all the flashes are. I make my way through the sea of cameras and microphones. Moments later, I get into a car. The door is slammed shut behind me.

Oscar later tells me that he was already exhausted when we entered the port. That from an emotional point of view, this mission has been very different from the other rescue operations he had been involved in. As for me, I sit there calmly when they put me in the vehicle and take me out of the port. However, it bothers me that they have taken me in this way in front of the refugees, and that they won't let me see what will happen to them. I don't know if they'll finally let them disembark. I didn't even get to say goodbye, only the boatswain managed to give me a quick hug before I was taken off the boat. It suddenly all happened very fast. I don't notice the cameras and shouts.

Bit by bit, everything the authorities have done – and everything they've failed to do – has narrowed down my options. In the end I had no choice but to act as I did, because I had to look after my passengers. By entering the port, I did nothing more than fulfil my obligation to save the people we'd rescued from the sea.

That's not a crime. But it isn't an act of heroism either.

With lives at stake, I believe the vast majority of captains would have made the same decision. And probably a lot of other people who have never been at sea as well.

I guess many still would have been frightened by the consequences. I, too, prefer to avoid conflict, but sometimes it's inevitable.

But if I think something matters, I'm not afraid to take responsibility.

None of my childhood experiences prepared me for this moment. I had a perfectly normal, middle-class – you could almost say boring – upbringing. I grew up in a small village in Lower Saxony near Celle, a batch of housing estates composed of single-family houses. There used to be an ammunition factory on the outskirts which employed forced labourers in World War II.

In the town stands a monument honouring the refugees from Prussia, Pomerania, Silesia, and the Sudetenland who found a new home here after the war and rebuilt the place from ruins. An interesting connection could be made – for those who wanted to make it – between my commitment to people who have lost their homes today and those displaced people who settled in my hometown. But this sort of resettlement was common across Germany, and it never occurred to me to think about it much.

As a child I loved being in nature. My parents' house was at the end of the road, and the garden backed onto the forest. I always climbed trees, the higher the better.

»Children like to play,« my mother used to say when her friends asked her why she let me clamber among the branches. »I can't keep forbidding her to do anything that seems dangerous. Life is full of risks, and that's just the way it is.«

My mother is a very pragmatic woman; if she had waited under the trees, watching me and worrying that I could fall, I might've never learned to trust my own judgement. I might've started to doubt myself. But climbing trees with no one to watch over me increased my confidence in my own abilities, as well as my appreciation for the nature around me. I liked to sit among the swaying treetops, usually in a larch or sometimes a chestnut tree. Back then, that was my only connection to nature.

I don't come from an environmentally conscious family. My father is an electrical engineer and worked for the German army for a long time, and later in the defence industry; my mother is an accountant. In my house there was no homemade muesli, my parents didn't take us to peace rallies and, as far as I know, they never chained themselves to railway tracks to block trains carrying nuclear waste. True, we didn't use plastic bags and we often ate vegetarian, but that was about as far as our environmentalism went.

We were not a high-consuming family, but that was mostly because we were often rather short on money; ever since I started primary school, my father had had phases of unemployment. There were times when my parents couldn't even pay the bank loans, and we almost sold the house. They rarely bought me clothes, and I didn't get as many Christmas presents as my friends.

To be honest, as a teenager I didn't think about doing things for others or committing myself to a cause. I was too busy with myself. Some kids in my class formed an local association supporting Greenpeace, but I wasn't interested in joining. I spent most of my teenage years in front of the computer. In my final three years of high school I did just three things: study, sleep, and play *World of Warcraft*. I spent a whole year online as one of its characters. I didn't just play the game, I stayed online to chat with other gamers.

My parents were worried that I was wasting my youth and undermining my prospects. That game may not have been the wisest way to spend my time, I admit, but I don't regret playing it. A video game that allows forty players to interact simultaneously is almost like a sports club with members competing for recognition and a spot on the team. Nowadays e-sports are much more accepted, although for me the real challenges are in the real world. Anyway, I had no idea what I wanted to do after high school. My father wanted me to be an engineer.

»Why don't you study political science?« a classmate of mine said to me one day. »That would suit you really well.«

»What makes you think that?« I replied, »It doesn't make any sense.«

Now, every time journalists ask me if I want to go into politics, I remember my high school classmate's words. Maybe she saw something in me that I wasn't aware of at the time. Then, the only thing that was clear to me was that I wanted to do something with tangible results, I wanted to work on something practical, not sit in an office all day. But it was a long time before I finally found a job that matched those criteria.

One day I heard there was a call for people to train for a specialty in nautical science; in other words, a job related to engineering. It sounded great because I'd always be on the move, I'd be working alone most of the time, and I wouldn't have to spend my days doing the same thing over and over.

The first semester of the course was practical. As students, we had to travel on a cargo ship carrying 8,000 containers. Our ship left Europe every two weeks and sailed through the Suez Canal to India and back. The round trip took about five weeks. I was bored by the endless watches from the bridge; the work schedule was rigid and didn't allow me any freedom. Many of my fellow students made no secret of the fact that they would rather be at home. By the time Christmas came, most of us were in a pretty bad mood and homesick. Our cook had been unable to attend the birth of his son.

Some took to drinking to drown their frustration. The end of their contracts – and therefore the date when they would be allowed to leave the ship – was constantly being postponed. Looking at all this, I couldn't help but wonder if I really wanted to continue studying nautical science and spend my life this way.

So, once the first theoretical semester of my studies was over, I decided to go abroad and think about my future. In Chile, I was hired as a tour guide on a ferry that sailed through the fjords and channels of Patagonia – a spectacular trip, as long as you weren't caught in the rain.

Every day we passed through Puerto Eden, a small town with a few houses huddled in the bay, behind which the majestic snow-capped mountains rise. It used to have about 800 inhabitants, mostly fishermen. But then the red tide arrived – a concentration of poisonous algae that stained the water the colour of blood. It killed all the seafood, leaving the people without a livelihood. Many were forced to abandon their homes.

You can find algal blooms in a range of locations across the Earth. They're a phenomenon caused by changes in temperature and wind direction, as well as the salinity of the water. They can be caused by warm waste water from power plants, and in some cases, by the El Niño current. When I arrived in Puerto Eden there were only seven Kawésqar, Indigenous people who were the first settlers of the southern Patagonian channels, and the population of the town had been reduced to a total of just over a hundred inhabitants.

In Chile I had been granted a year-long work visa, paid for by the shipping company, and when my contract ended I travelled the continent – mainly Argentina and Peru – and learned Spanish. When I returned to Germany I thought about enrolling in a different degree programme, but a friend convinced me that it would be better to complete my nautical science studies. In an effort to graduate as soon as possible, I compiled a syllabus with all the outstanding subjects and, in order to make up for lost time, enrolled in twice as many courses and exams as usual.

I spent the second semester of my internship on a ship belonging to the German Ministry of Education and Research. The *Meteor* employs scientists and researchers from various fields, from oceanography and marine biology to sedimentology. The navigating officers had much more interesting work to do than on the cargo ship, the crew's social backgrounds were much more diverse, and everyone shared the spirit of research. I worked with a former naval officer who was experienced in training personnel. We got along well instantly and, despite the teasing of the rest of the colleagues, on our shift he always left me, a non-smoker, indoors, and went outside to light up.

»This week I'll teach you everything we do here,« he said, »then you'll drive the ship and I'll watch.«

And that's how I really learned a lot.

Above all, I learned how to take responsibility, and how to take on difficult tasks.

I knew right then that this was what I wanted to do with my life – to sail – but not necessarily as a captain. Captains have to do mountains of paperwork, and that's really not my thing. I've done a lot of different jobs, so it's strange to me that some people reduce my life's journey to the 21 days I was captain of *Sea-Watch 3*.

In my native German, I refer to my job title as »*Kapitän*«, not »*Kapitänin*«, in the feminine, because I don't like the latter term. The correct professional designation is »*Kapitän*«. I'm fully aware of the fact that I'm a woman.

I tend to feel a bit out of place among merchant ship captains, especially as more than two years have now gone by since I've been at sea in a professional capacity. But right now I don't need a captain's certificate to sail, because the *Sea-Watch 3* is a yacht and subject to different rules. What matters much more is experience.

After the *Meteor*, I spent the second part of the semester on the *MS Transrussia*, one of the two North Sea ferries linking Lübeck and St Petersburg twice a week. It's a typical merchant ship, designed to carry heavy goods vehicles, not passengers.

The captain was close to retirement. He was a kind, serious man with long experience in ice navigation. Crossing the sea ice is an art form, especially when it snows, or in the middle of the night when you can't see anything at all. It's also a fantastic feeling: when the ice breaks, you hear a cracking sound, which I find deeply satisfying. When I sail on ice, I sleep well, though sometimes the boat shakes a little as it breaks through the floes. But most beautiful of all were the sunrises before we reached St Petersburg. I usually spent the night on the bridge, so that when the sun rose in the east I could see all the ships in front of me slowly making their way through the ice floes like a caravan.

Due to the harsh conditions, we often came across ships trapped in the ice. Our ferry had a high ice class, meaning that it was very strong thanks to the distance between the frames and the thickness of the steel, so it could pass through thick ice. I loved sailing across the icy surface, and even learned how to operate the rudder and engines to free the ship in case we got stuck.

The *Transrussia* and the *Meteor* were from the same shipping company, and they had already confirmed that they were willing to take me on as soon as I finished my studies. However, not wanting to end up on a freighter again, I asked the head of HR to assign me to one of the research vessels. Shortly before my graduation exam, he sent me an email:

»On 4 August, there is a vacancy on the *Polarstern* that you could fill.«

It does pay to ask. Although it may seem like a normal job, for me it was like winning the lottery. I was overjoyed: *Polarstern*, Germany's polar research vessel! Every navigator dreams of working there; I wanted to even more after discovering my passion for ice.

I was under a lot of pressure, because to get the job I first had to pass the qualifying exam.

But I did it. At the time I couldn't have guessed the Arctic expedition was going to be one of the most formative experiences of my life, and not only my professional life. I was just overjoyed to be on the ice. The *Polarstern* is a rather special icebreaker that sails in the Arctic in the northern summer, and in the Antarctic in the southern summer, following the relative warmth and thinner ice. In 2019, the *Polarstern* headed to the Arctic for a full year, drifting through the ice, allowing the ship to get stuck in the floes at times and then break free. In all other expeditions, we'd simply break through the ice. And I had some experience with that from working on the ferry.

But I wasn't prepared for what I would see in the Arctic Ocean.

As it happened, when we reached the North Pole itself, I was on shift. That morning I was watch-keeping on the bridge, while the captain, who had been on *Polarstern*'s two previous expeditions to the North Pole, remained in the background. At the North Pole you can't see land for miles around. You can only establish your position from the co-ordinates.

The ice was white instead of bluish, full of air pockets, and the floes were thin. The researchers couldn't set up their scientific equipment to make measurements because the ice wasn't strong enough. They needed ice that was multiple years old.

»This is first-year ice,« the captain told me. »Never seen it in this area before. Twenty years ago we were here together with a Swedish icebreaker and it was hard to get through. Now, there's hardly any ice at all.« It took us half an hour of cruising with a helicopter to find older ice.

»In my lifetime alone, I've seen less and less ice,« said Sergey, one of the Russian oceanographers. The scientist leading the expedition was also concerned about these rapid changes. I was shocked, but reassured that there was a whole team of competent scientists working on it. We were part of a system for collecting reliable scientific data, and that had to be of some use, didn't it?

I crewed five *Polarstern* missions. I soon learned how to steer the ship; it was something I enjoyed. You have to steer carefully there, and you're almost always alone on the bridge. Sometimes, in order to get a good view of the ice floes and find the best route, I had stop the ship and climb up to the »crow's nest«, the observation platform ten metres above the bridge. It's the only way to see the ice floes in the distance and plot a course to pass slowly between them. Travelling through ice floes, the ship slows down or sometimes gets stuck. So it usually saves time to take the long route around large ice floes.

If a strong wind blows and all the ice sheets push in one direction and compact, there's no space left to sail between them. The ship is stranded, and all you can do is wait for the wind to change direction, as sailors did in the old days. I was never bored on the ship, as there were several scientific teams, most of them always eager to explain what they were doing and what the data they were collecting would be utilised for. With their meticulous research, they put together tiny pieces of a huge and complicated jigsaw puzzle which, once completed, would bring new insights.

Time passed quickly.

Everyone was satisfied with the work I was doing.

The only one who wasn't completely satisfied was me.

Because we were running out of time. The research didn't seem to actually change anything. Everyone was debating, weighing up data, writing up scientific studies and reports for politicians. But our leaders did nothing. They didn't pass climate policy measures to prevent the poles from melting. To me, the research seemed increasingly pointless, and I felt dissatisfied serving as a kind of chauffeur for research teams. I felt I wasn't putting my energy in the right place.

Also, I wanted to work on my own rather than for others – and I wanted to spend more time in nature. In between *Polarstern* missions, I did a lot of travelling, for instance across South America and Pakistan, where I spent much of my time camping. I just liked being out in nature, enjoying the great outdoors. When I returned to the icebreaker, the bridge seemed to me like an office – albeit one with a spectacular view of frozen mountains. In other words, I wanted to do something hands-on to halt the destruction of nature, even if that would mean doing it only on a very small scale. So I left my job at the *Polarstern*. It was clear to me that I couldn't continue my work there and that I had to try something different.

I signed up for a European volunteer programme and worked for eight months in the Bystrinsky Nature Park in the far east of Russia. It's a large stretch of birch and coniferous forests, plagued by mosquitoes in the summer. We had to walk long distances on foot, as there were hardly any paved roads. In July the grasses grew so tall that when I was on a pony, they brushed my saddle. The park was rather understaffed, with only seven regular employees and a few volunteers, who included a German cartographer, a Latvian anthropologist, and a Russian geo-ecologist called Ksenia, whom I often helped. She had worked for several years for the oil industry and wanted to return to biology.

As for actual conservation, I didn't learn as much as I'd hoped; we were too busy repairing huts, felling trees, and cutting firewood for the winter, which took up all the time we could have spent on the real work of environmental conservation. Moreover, it's not easy to work in such vast and often impassable terrain: sometimes it took three days to reach a place that was less than seventy kilometres away; our vehicles broke down frequently, and the rangers were often more mechanics than environmental custodians.

Once, on our travels to record the plant life of the area, we visited a family living in a secluded hut. They were part of the Evens, hunters and reindeer herders indigenous to Northeastern Siberia. But what impressed me most was the forest in that place, forest in a natural, primeval state, the likes of which I had never seen before and have never seen since in Europe.

After eight months in Bystrinsky I wanted to do something that would have political impact, so I went to work on a Greenpeace vessel. As a navigator, I didn't have a very good time. I didn't actually want to be a navigator any longer; I was bored on the bridge. I found what the Greenpeace activists were doing far more interesting. They investigated possible illegal fishing, they knew fishing legislation inside out, they planned campaigns, and connected organisations and people.

One of the German volunteers told me about a new organisation called Sea-Watch, which was rescuing refugees shipwrecked in the Mediterranean. She had friends who worked there, and they told her that they urgently needed support. So I wrote them an email offering my help. Despite sending several more emails, I didn't hear back; I wouldn't find out until much later that Sea-Watch was overwhelmed with enquiries at the time, but they didn't have a proper organisational structure and their few volunteers couldn't handle all the incoming emails.

In the autumn of 2015, I enrolled in a Masters in Environmental Conservation in Ormskirk, a modest market town north of Liverpool. At the time, the refugee situation in Greece was worsening. During the winter, the island of Lesbos had become the entry point for many refugees arriving from the Middle East, the vast majority from Syria, around 18 % from Afghanistan, and 3 % from Pakistan. Day and night, boats with refugees were arriving on the small Greek island, at its height at a rate of about 3,000 a day. According to UNHCR figures, some 390,000 had arrived by the end of that year.

Greece still bears the lion's share of the burden that should be borne by Europe. At the time that I'm writing this book, 2019, some 8,000 refugees live in Mória, the infamous refugee camp; it was built to accommodate 2,500. According to Médecins Sans Frontières, it is »the worst refugee camp in the world«, suffering from horrific hygiene conditions, a high barbed-wire fence, conflicts with the locals, and a lack of adequate heating and running water. Suicide attempts and violence are common.

I didn't hear much about it. I was absorbed in my studies, not to mention my ongoing infection with the »polar virus«: my fascination with the eternal ice which, I was beginning to grasp, was far from eternal.

To continue working in that environment without abandoning my studies, I applied for a job with the British Antarctic Survey, the UK's official Antarctic research institution. However, I still found the work on the ship tedious. It became increasingly clear to me that I didn't want to keep working as a navigator.

We were in the last week of one of the scientific expeditions, and just as we were returning to the Falkland Islands

I received an email from Sea-Watch. At that point I was no longer expecting to hear from them. But it turned out that a captain had fallen ill at the last moment, and they needed someone who could join the mission immediately. An emergency, so I agreed to help out.

It was the second mission for the *Sea-Watch 2*.

I had no idea what to expect.

I was only given a short technical handover.

I knew nothing about Sea-Watch, and even less about the situation in the Mediterranean.

To make matters worse, there were so many volunteers on board that it was a bit chaotic. I was captain and boatswain in one, as I also had to take care of maintenance and organisation on deck. Even so, I enjoyed the work because we were a team; everyone was motivated, was keen to help, keen to learn.

Apart from me, there were only two crew members who knew anything about seafaring. We only met each other on the boat; we were a small team, thirteen people on their first mission together. *Sea-Watch 2* has rescued more than 25,000 refugees. It's an old boat that holds up well in the water and was much smaller than most of the boats I had sailed on before.

Because I was happy and involved in something that I found meaningful, I worked two missions in a row. At the time, we rescued shipwrecked people and handed them over to Italian coastguards, EU military vessels, or Frontex patrols. We would wait by the boats and hand out life jackets. We only took people on board when we had no other choice, like when we took aboard 130 refugees from an inflatable dinghy before aiding a wooden barge that had capsized nearby.

We had plenty of work. There were weeks when several vessels capsized, and most of the occupants who make the crossing are exhausted and can't swim. On one occasion, an Italian military ship asked for help because they were essentially only pulling bodies out of the water. They asked helpers on speedboats to mark the bodies with life jackets. It was there that a now well-known photo was taken of one of our volunteers, Martin Kolek, holding a dead baby in his arms.

»I was prepared to see people drowning,« he said later. »But still, the reality is very different. I was prepared for many things, but I wasn't expecting my worldview to shift this dramatically.«

It's very depressing to witness dead bodies being pulled out of the water merely because we were a few hours – sometimes, just a few minutes – too late.

Should I quit my job at the British Antarctic Survey? On the one hand, what we were doing in the Mediterranean was important; on the other, small vessels can be driven without a merchant shipping licence, so there were usually plenty of captains available.

Nature conservation was even more important to me, precisely because it receives far less attention than humanitarian disaster relief – including Mediterranean rescues. So I dedicated myself to conservation and didn't free up time to help with rescues again until the summer of 2017. This time I joined Sea-Eye, the organisation that now operates the rescue ship *Alan Kurdi*; a boat named after the Syrian boy whose drowned body was washed up on a beach in

Turkey. I sailed on the *Seefuchs*, also taking command of one of the semi-rigid rescue boats because I didn't want to just stand around on the bridge. That same summer, Sea-Watch asked me if I could help prepare *Sea-Watch 3*, the ship they had just acquired.

I spent two months on the ship, long working days, filled with technical inspections and all the paperwork involved in changing the flag state. It took much longer than expected to get the necessary documents, which was frustrating because the ship was supposed to have been at sea, saving lives, long ago.

While I was in the midst of these preparations, in August the Italian authorities in Lampedusa confiscated the *Iuventa*, a boat belonging to an NGO called Jugend Rettet. I wasn't too surprised, as I'd already spoken to a colleague back in the spring about the possibility of this kind of political repression. Still, the news marked a turning point: we realised that sea rescue was now being criminalised. Public opinion suddenly shifted; there were more and more accusations that sea rescue teams were in cahoots with human traffickers.

I spent the winter doing field research for my master's thesis in south Georgia in sub-Antarctica. The subject was – among other things – the rehabilitation of ecosystems, observing how the local seal populations recovered after having been almost completely eradicated by humans.

During my studies I became increasingly aware that the main threat to biodiversity is not climate collapse, but our use of land and exploitation of resources. Or rather, in the over-consumption of the industrialised countries. Because I had some spare time the following summer, I returned to the Mediterranean. However, I didn't want to spend any time at sea, so I volunteered to help the team on the rescue plane. I had been supporting Sea-Watch by plane since the end of 2017; and on the *Polarstern* I had flown in the helicopter with my colleagues.

Today, rescue operations in the central Mediterranean are mainly conducted from the air. The EU military regularly monitors the sea, often from bases on Lampedusa or Malta, and the European Border and Coast Guard Agency, Frontex, uses drones and aircraft, too – one is called *Seagull*. Ideally, we fly out in two small civilian aircraft named *Moonbird* and *Colibri*. Sea-Watch oversees tactical coordination, but the aircraft and pilots are provided by another organisation.

It isn't easy for rescue vessels to detect refugee boats, because they're so small that you only spot them at close range. Most of the dinghies sail from a very long stretch of coastline. Usually none of the occupants carries a compass, so they navigate as best they can by the constellations or, for the lucky ones, using the GPS on someone's mobile phone. But they also have to reckon with ocean currents and wind, which can blow them off course.

Finding a boat sighted a few hours earlier by the *Moonbird* is quite difficult. No one knows how fast the dinghy is travelling, or whether it is actually sailing towards the nearest European port. The boats are often sailing in the wrong direction, or their engines are cut off and they drift. Finding them is like finding a needle in a haystack, and it's also a race against time, because dinghies like these can sink at any moment. The planes scan the entire coastline, as there could always be more people risking a dangerous crossing to Europe. But because their fuel supply is limited, they can only spend a few hours searching from the air.

Rescue operations this year were facing an increasingly difficult situation. Political repression became evident: *Lifeline* was confiscated. *Sea-Watch 3* was held in Valletta for an alleged violation of its legal registration, *Seefuchs* encountered similar problems. NGOs such as SOS, Médecins Sans Frontières and Save the Children stopped their humanitarian missions because they weren't getting enough donations, and rescue workers were questioned by the police as soon as they came ashore. A Code of Conduct was put into force that imposed on us stricter regulations at sea and additional obligations. The Netherlands suddenly introduced a set of brand-new regulations on rescue vessels, which, among other things, entailed more inspections. Italy passed a decree banning civilian rescue ships from its territorial waters. We were forced to refuel *Moonbird* in Tunisia, which was absurd given the extra mileage involved.

The new regulations made life for us more difficult. And led to even more deaths at sea.

When I left shore with *Sea-Watch 3* in June 2019, I was aware that the tense political situation in Italy might lead the public prosecutor's office to open an investigation against us. Xenophobic political parties had come to power the previous year, partly thanks to the EU's lack of solidarity on immigration. Preliminary investigations had already been opened against several other captains, and had then been closed. But none of that made me back down, because I was and remain firmly convinced that we, as a civil society, cannot leave Europe's external borders and the definition of human rights exposed to right-wing nationalists like those at the head of the Italian Interior Ministry. We must not allow ourselves to be intimidated. That's why I felt morally obliged to undertake this journey; simply because I could, even if I wasn't too keen about being at sea anymore.

Saving lives is a humanitarian imperative.

It always will be.

We must give aid and support to each other.

As much as we can.

To the weakest first.

The German theologian Martin Niemöller, initially a supporter of Hitler but later an active member of the resistance and, after the war, of the peace movement, wrote a poem that reflects powerfully on why those of us who are in the majority must protect the rights of minorities, such as refugees.

When the Nazis came for the communists, I did not speak out; I was not a communist.

When they locked up the social democrats, I did not speak out; I was not a social democrat.

When they came for the trade unionists, I did not speak out; I was not a trade unionist.

When they came for me, there was no one left to speak out.

As long as we continue to think of people in need as »the others« and look the other way instead of helping them, our civilisation will lack a North Star. Freedom of expression and the right to life are two fundamental human rights. We cannot look the other way simply because violations affect groups we don't feel attached to. That erodes the human rights we all lay claim to; the weakest just feel them eroding first.

In my view, everyone who has a position of privilege has an obligation to use it on behalf of others.

Those who have rights are in a lucky position. But then you have a responsibility to help those ignored by the system.

Chapter Three:
The last generation?

We're going to the police station.«
The commander of the Guardia di Finanza looks angry. Maybe he's upset about the scratches on his patrol boat, or maybe it's the situation itself. His colleague turns the ignition and we drive off, leaving behind the harbour lights.

I knew I was in for a long night somewhere, but it hadn't occurred to me that it might be at the customs station. Apparently what I did out of necessity, because the authorities and European politicians were dodging their responsibilities, has led to exactly the legal complications I had feared.

Shortly afterwards, the vehicle stops in front of a modest two-storey building where journalists are already waiting. One of the customs officials leads me inside and asks me to take a seat. It is a sober space, with no pictures on the walls and no plants anywhere; just two tables, a computer, a printer, a couple of chairs, and a bookshelf filled with dossiers and legal codes.

We're waiting for my lawyer, who arrives in a hurry twenty minutes later. He looks worried.

The officials spend a long time typing their report on the computer and discussing the legal articles I've allegedly contravened. In the meantime, my lawyer discusses my situation with them. As they speak in Italian, I try to follow the conversation, but I don't understand much. The head of the customs police offers us all an espresso.

I hold back my yawns as best I can and keep looking at my watch, whose hands seem to be moving in slow motion. I am tired. I'd like to sleep, but a nagging worry keeps me awake.

When I was being taken off *Sea-Watch 3* amidst both angry shouts and applause, when the police put me in the back seat of the vehicle waiting on the quay, I had only one thing on my mind: »Fuck, now I won't know what's going to happen on the ship.«

I keep asking the customs officials if they let the rescued people disembark.

So far there's no news. Little by little, it's becoming clear that I won't be able to return to the boat. It's just emerged that it will indeed be confiscated by the Public Prosecutor's Office, and the officials are now arguing about who has to take it out of the port. It's highly unlikely that I'll be allowed to take *Sea-Watch 3* out of the dock; the media would be all over me as soon as I set foot in the harbour, and I assume the customs officials are afraid of looking ridiculous. There's a lot of paperwork to complete, and they end up printing out the reports several times because they keep finding mistakes. They, too, are tired.

»Good, now we'll collect the refugees from the ship,« says the head of customs at five o'clock in the morning.

It's about time. They need to get the ship off the dock before six o'clock so the airport can begin operation. The crew can definitely manage without me, but I would have liked to say goodbye. Now that the refugees have disembarked, the crew will probably take some time to rest. Then it's likely that someone will have to take the ship to the port of Licata, which we left seventeen days ago.

I think about all this as I shift restlessly back and forth in my chair.

The head of customs examines the reports again, turns the pages, looks up. He lifts his coffee cup to his lips before putting it back on the saucer – it's already empty. He shakes his head and lets out a groan.

He must be annoyed. I guess he was expecting an uncomplicated job, and now he's dealing with an issue of international politics.

I don't mind being arrested for having complied with maritime law, but the procedure is proving onerous. I just hope that all this hassle will finally do some good: If Italy's new law is debated in court, it can be ruled as a violation of existing law. Then it can be invalidated.

I'm going to be kept under house arrest until the hearing takes place, because they don't have a prison on Lampedusa. The hearing can't take place until Monday, because today is Saturday and the court is, of course, closed for the weekend. If you told someone that in 2019, a person was arrested in Europe for saving lives, they'd be shocked. It doesn't say anything good about our community of nations that more and more right-wing rhetoric finds its way into our laws and actions. There shouldn't be any question about taking in people in desperate need. We shouldn't just help them to reach a safe harbour, we should also treat them with dignity and respect when they arrive on our shores. It should be clear to everyone; after all, it's a fundamental principle enshrined in the constitutions of many European countries.

The way refugees are being treated in states that consider themselves civilised cannot be tolerated. Ever larger and more inhumane camps are being built.

The people are being forgotten, like they are in Mória.

Mistreated, like in Calais, where the police pepper-spray the refugees' food supplies and slash their tents at night.

Shot, like the refugees at the Bulgarian border.

The way people are treated and mistreated, the speedy trials at which their status is decided, the appalling conditions in the camps that make so many despair and eventually end their lives – all of this shows that human rights don't apply equally to all people in the European Union.

The conditions these people face on their journey are becoming a serious threat to an ever growing number of them. In the future, more and more people will be forced to leave their homes due to ecological disasters and economic deprivation. This is a fact, studies have made this abundantly clear. People often say that we need to improve conditions in their home countries to stop people from leaving their homes, or cut off migration routes, but this only shows that people haven't understood the issue. We can't solve this problem by acting in their home countries or along their migration routes alone, because that's not where the problem originates.

The causes of migration are complex, often there are many reasons why people leave their country. But we must be clear that if someone decides to leave their home, it's because they don't have a choice.

One of the reasons people migrate is because of the changing climatic and ecological conditions on our planet. According to a report by the Internal Displacement Monitoring Centre (IDMC), in the first half of 2019 alone, seven million people were displaced within their own country because of floods, such as in the Philippines, Ethiopia, Bolivia, and Iran, or because of cyclones such as Fani, which hit the Bay of Bengal on the east coast of India, or Idai, which hit East Africa.

People flee such natural disasters because they can't survive on the devastated land. They usually leave in a hurry, but don't go far, and if possible they typically return as soon as possible to rebuild their homes if they can somehow find the money and materials. While natural disasters such as typhoons and hurricanes have always occurred, science shows that climate change is making these extreme weather events more frequent and severe. In the future, they will displace even more people from their homes.

More and more people are going to be driven from their homes by expanding environmental destruction. Industry pollutes the air and poisons the drinking water, while industrial agriculture destroys the nutrients in the soil and erodes the land. Adding to this are the effects of the climate crisis, like salinisation of farmland, rising sea levels, lack of rainfall or increased droughts, and flooding in coastal areas as glaciers melt. When people leave their homes for these reasons, we call it »forced migration«.

These people often are subsistence farmers, so pollution or degradation of their homeland instantly becomes a problem, and eventually a disaster. They can no longer live on what they produce; that's why migrating is often the only option they're left with. This is a reaction to food shortages, to poverty and unemployment, to conflicts, which are often exacerbated by the already massively more difficult conditions. In Syria, for example, one of the factors that triggered the civil war was a drought that destroyed crops and raised the price of bread by 90 %.

People suffering these problems often seek work elsewhere in their country, and many end up in the slums and shanty towns of large cities. They are considered internally displaced people (IDPs). Only a fraction move to neighbouring countries, and even fewer cross borders further afield.

If they find their way to Europe, they have little chance of staying by legal means as »economic refugees«. The Geneva Convention relating to the Status of Refugees only recognises asylum seekers as individuals who are persecuted on account of their ethnicity, religion, membership of a social group, or political opinion. Officially, there are no climate refugees, even though many UN documents and resolutions warn of climate-induced migration.

Various UN institutions and negotiating panels are looking for ways to protect the rights of climate migrants. »Climate change will have devastating consequences for people in poverty,« notes the 2019 UN report on Climate Change and Poverty, to take one example. »Even under the best-case scenario, hundreds of millions will face food insecurity, forced migration, disease and death. Climate change threatens the future of human rights and risks undoing the last 50 years of progress in development, global health and poverty reduction.« The Global Compact for Safe, Orderly and Regular Migration (GCM), adopted in 2018 by the UN, clearly spells out the link between climate change and migration. However, this pact isn't legally binding. It's not just that there's little political will to protect climate refugees, there's also no clear institutional commitment to the issue. One possible solution would be to include climate-related migration in the UN Framework Convention on Climate Change, which, unlike the GCM, is legally binding and already has a »Taskforce on Displacement« addressing this and related issues. However, there's still a long way to go before concrete measures are adopted, such as »climate passports«, i. e. passports issued to climate refugees granting them citizenship rights in safe states, or the recognition of climate change as grounds for asylum.

It's unacceptable that international law hasn't recognised climate change as a cause of migration, and that those affected by it aren't defined as refugees by the Geneva Refugee Convention. Industrialised countries obviously have little interest in a fairer world. The governments of states that refuse to take in refugees, the managers of oil and energy companies, and the powerful people in finance clearly have a share of responsibility for the situation, as consumerism and energy consumption and the associated emissions of the Global North are the root cause of many of these environmental problems.

Richer states, instead of taking responsibility, are walling themselves in, preventing or obstructing migration as much as they can by interring refugees close to borders and sending them back. Those who treat migrants this way are partly responsible for the many deaths among refugees. You can't scare people into staying at home when their lives were already at risk there.

It's not the refugees who cause a crisis, but those who want to stop them from leaving their countries. We're not facing a refugee crisis. We're facing a justice crisis. If there were safe escape routes, or if people could apply for residence permits or asylum while in their countries of origin, we wouldn't have deaths in the Mediterranean or in the Sahara, and there wouldn't be human traffickers profiting from those fearing for their lives.

There's only one way to address this justice crisis: we need to reframe migration – as an integral part of life, fresh momentum for societies, a human right, and as an undeniable reality in a radically changing world. Migration actually brings benefits to societies, for instance by creating forums to exchange ideas, and the money sent home by migrants exceeds the money spent on foreign aid and actually reaches the people who really need it.

There shouldn't just be a right to flee; it also must be properly implemented. Instead of criminalising migrants, we need to help them settle among us, and we need to recognise our responsibility for the circumstances that led to their flight.

There is constant talk of the need to »combat«, »eliminate«, or »limit« the causes of migration. This is ridiculous, because at no point have the real causes of migration been addressed: the climate crisis and the collapse of our ecosystems.

It's the big polluters – us in the industrialised countries – who have completely unbalanced the Earth's climate.

From a science perspective, there's not a shred of doubt: 99 % of climate scientists say that today's warming world is the result of human activity. Since the industrial revolution, the Earth's average temperature has risen by 1.1 °C. This change is bad enough in itself, but worryingly, all the scenarios used by the Intergovernmental Panel on Climate Change (IPCC) are based on the now untenable assumption that global warming is a linear process.

Only now is the general public beginning to realise that these rapid changes are beyond our control. Recent studies lay this out in detail, and the melting ice in Greenland and Antarctica, which is heating two to three times faster than the rest of the planet, is a further indicator: global warming doesn't follow a straight line, but an exponential one; and once a certain threshold is reached, the process is irreversible.

This is because everything on Earth is interrelated and mutually dependent. In the Earth's climate system, there are tipping elements that could set in motion so-called »positive feedback effects«. Once triggered, they could set off cascades of tipping points in other elements and result in unchecked global heating.

Summer sea ice in the Arctic is one of the most vulnerable elements on Earth, and scientists estimate that its tipping point would be reached with just two degrees of global heating. The ice has been shrinking rapidly for decades, not just covering less area but also growing thinner. Researchers expect the Arctic to be ice-free in summer by 2035.

Already today, the melting is accelerating because of a positive feedback mechanism called the ice albedo feedback mechanism. Basically, as large masses of white ice melt, they produce more water surfaces. The shrinking white ice shelves then reflect less sunlight, while the water absorbs more of the sun's heat and warms the surrounding ice floes.

These in turn thaw, exposing more dark surfaces. Which in turn causes the ice to heat even more.

As the water in the oceans warms, the ice masses also thaw from below. Moreover, in many places the ice is stained with dust and soot, and even encrusted with pigments from microalgae and bacteria. The ice therefore becomes darker and absorbs more of the sun's heat – melting even faster.

All these mutually reinforcing effects cause the Arctic to warm twice as fast as the rest of the Earth. Other tipping elements go through similar processes. The West Antarctic ice sheet, Alpine glaciers, and coral reefs are all about as vulnerable as the ice in Greenland. Gradually, the boreal coniferous forests, the Amazon rainforest, the thermohaline circulation (also known as the global ocean conveyor belt), the jet stream, the Indian summer monsoon and, eventually, the permafrost and the East Antarctic ice sheet would also be »tipped«.

In addition, the loss of countless ecosystems, such as annihilated coral reefs or the expanding Sahel desert, can cause positive feedback effects.

These tipping elements could act like dominoes, each triggering the next. Together, they could cause an additional four to six degrees Celsius of heating by the end of the century. Facing changes this dramatic, we can't afford to wait until we know everything there is to know. The opposite is the case: our guiding principle needs to be precaution, in the way it's applied in health and environmental policy, where it's intended to prevent irreversible damage. It consists of two strands, risk prevention and sustainable resource management. A precautionary approach to managing risks means acting before the damage is done, even if we don't know exactly how much environmental damage we're facing, how extensive it will be, how likely each scenario is to happen, or how different environmental impacts are related to each other, because all these losses must be avoided. Taking a precautionary approach to resource management means that we have to use natural elements such as water, land, and air sustainably to make sure they'll be there for the next generations. The precautionary principle has proved extremely useful, for example in the definition of protected areas, or in the Montreal Protocol, the agreement on the protection of the ozone layer.

The precautionary principle is enshrined in the Earth Charter promoted by the United Nations; in the environmental laws of countries such as Switzerland and Germany; in the Rio Declaration on Environment and Development; in the Treaty of Rome that established the European Community. In other words, it's part and parcel of European legislation. The devastating climate policies of individual nations, however, are clearly proof that it's far from being implemented.

Throughout the Earth's history there have been phases of extreme climate change, such as the transition that took place 34 million years ago after a long period of tropical warming and marked the beginning of an ice age. They all had a fundamental impact on life on our planet.

Now, it is us humans who are responsible for the biological, geological, and atmospheric processes that are destroying our planet, which is why some researchers call our era the Anthropocene – the Age of Humans. But as humans, we've only just started to realise the impact we're having on the environment. Right now, it doesn't look like the Anthropocene will be a particularly long era. Instead, it might just turn out to be a short blip at the onset of the sixth mass extinction.

It is an illusion that keeps being sold to us: The adaptation to the rising temperature is only possible up to a point – irrespective of whether that's by means of migration or technical solutions that will only be available to the wealthier part of humanity. Because the human body has a tolerance threshold when it comes to heat. Extreme temperatures lead to hyperthermia: The body cannot release the warmth, is no longer able to cool itself and just absorbs heat. If hyperthermia persists too long it can be fatal.

Many people in temperate zones don't yet realise the danger. But across the world, many deaths are already being attributed to climate change. What is clear is that the people who have contributed the least to this disaster are the ones who will suffer the earliest and most severely, and that what is at stake here is therefore climate justice. A two degree Celsius increase means even more extreme weather, especially in the Global South where most countries have limited resources to deal with floods, droughts, and storms. People in these regions often have no housing insurance, no public health services, and no emergency service infrastructure.

The 2012 Climate Vulnerability Monitor showed that the climate crisis isn't just causing financial harm (mainly in terms of infrastructure damage), but also that climate change and fossil fuels are already causing around five million deaths per year. These deaths occur mainly in countries in the Global South, but all nations are affected by the climate emergency. According to the latest estimates, there could be six million deaths every year by 2030.

The reports and papers coming from the world's climate research institutes clearly show that our window of opportunity to act on the climate crisis is small, and that it will be difficult to stop the Earth from heating more than two degrees Celsius. Without radical changes to our economy and way of life, we will blow the remaining »carbon budget« we have to avoid 1.5 °C heating in just eight years – and that »budget« already assumes that we'll be making extensive use of negative emissions technology. So while the 1.5 °C target is still achievable in theory, it seems like a distant dream given the decades of inaction and current policies. This should jolt us into action immediately.

But so far there isn't a sensible international strategy to avoid collapse.

Instead, we're witnessing political failure. Since 1995, international delegates from the realms of science and politics have met annually to discuss the importance of climate change. The most recent political turning point was the climate conference in Paris in 2015, where the world agreed to limit global warming to 1.5 °C, or at most, 2 °C.

The UN Framework Convention on Climate Change negotiations, which produced the Paris outcome, are doomed to failure unless they ask the right questions and, building on honest answers, draw the necessary conclusions. So long as the negotiating states ask questions framed by the logic of the existing economic system, they will be the wrong questions, because it's the logic of this economic system that created these problems in the first place. The Paris proposals are based on the IPCC scenarios, which are widely considered rather conservative. This means that even if we were to meet the Paris climate targets, we still wouldn't be sufficiently protected from the effects of the climate crisis. Quite apart from the fact that people are already dying as a result of rising temperatures.

So far, no country has made serious changes as a result of the Paris Agreement. On the contrary, the former president of one of the most polluting countries in the world – both in terms of its energy production and use, and the consumption of products imported from countries such as China – withdrew from the agreement. Almost all governments plan to increase their gross domestic product (GDP), to further exploit nature, and to subsidise highly polluting companies. For most people in politics, economic growth is more important than protecting the planet – even if it costs the Earth itself.

The Paris Agreement is also based on the idea that geo-engineering can remove carbon dioxide from the atmosphere, either by managing solar radiation or by absorbing carbon dioxide. One of the currently most-hyped ways to absorb carbon dioxide is Bioenergy with Carbon Capture and Storage (BECCS). This means cultivating fast-growing plants, burning those plants to create energy, and capturing and storing the carbon dioxide generated in the process. But BECCS doesn't solve the problem, because to have sufficient impact, immense areas of land would have to be planted with fast-growing monocultures, destroying biodiversity and claiming gigantic fields. Any intervention in nature carries risks. None of these climate technologies exists at the scale needed – and implementing them would be a very risky global experiment.

It's frightening but unsurprising that fossil-fuel companies are pouring money into climate engineering research, to delay the transition away from fossil fuels for as long as possible. Critics consider geoengineering and other so-called climate protection methods that come with a high risk of environmental destruction – or even human rights violations – to be »false solutions«.

It becomes clear that politics and the economy are powerful allies that cause even the most reasonable initiatives to fail. Consumers and political decision-makers have been duped by corporations for decades. As the extensive research by historians of science Naomi Oreskes and Eric Conway shows, it was primarily the oil industry, but also car manufacturers, who invested millions of dollars in research and marketing designed to cast doubt on the human-induced climate crisis and the effects of the carbon dioxide produced by humans – in some cases aided by the same public relations consultants who cast doubt on the harmful effects of tobacco, the dangers of the ozone hole, or the damage caused by the insecticide DDT.

Due to obfuscation and political inaction, we have reached a point in which all we can do is limit the damage. We have entered a grey zone between bad and worse.

When climate scientists say this, some people, often called »doomers«, interpret this as meaning that it's too late, and that it's no use doing anything. But then, we rarely hear an honest word from parliamentarians, from the people who either profit from the current system because they sit on a company board, or are genuinely convinced that small steps will suffice to avert disaster.

They're acting in the interests of the economy, and some probably believe they're acting in the general interest. So, since the 2015 Paris Agreement, we've seen the exact opposite of what we were promised; annual carbon dioxide emissions have increased since the negotiations began, from 360 ppm in 2015 to 415 ppm in 2019. Our climate system is changing at a terrifying rate, permafrost is thawing, glaciers are melting and disappearing, ever-increasing heat waves, floods, and storms are killing people. More species have died out. More forests have been cut down. More rivers have been polluted, more plastic has been washed into our oceans. More people are leaving their countries.

We can see changes in the biosphere almost everywhere on Earth. We've wiped out a lot of ecosystems, and we're now discovering that destroyed ecosystems can't buffer today's extreme weather.

Many species have been decimated by our exploitation of nature, through habitat loss, or the fragmentation of landscapes as trees are cut down to produce soy or palm oil, through pesticides from agriculture and industrial wastewater, and through overfishing and overhunting. The average population numbers of vertebrates – and these are the only ones for which sufficient data are available – declined by 60 % between 1970 and 2014, according to the WWF Living Planet Report. There is no reversal of this distressing trend in sight; populations are shrinking by an average of two percent every year. By mass, 96 % of all vertebrates on Earth today are humans and our livestock.

The extinction rate today is a thousand times higher than the background rate, i. e. the rate at which species tend to disappear. Normally, this takes up to ten million years.

Since colonial times, Indigenous peoples, although they have the smallest impact on nature of any of us, have been the first and worst affected by the destruction of nature.

They often live directly from the land and sea, and their territories protect 80 % of the world's biodiversity. Rather than getting the chance to teach us about nature's web of life, they are murdered or resettled to open national parks and build oil pipelines. They suffer the most from pollution, when, as in Russia, about 10 % of the oil produced is lost from pipeline spillages or, as in Nigeria, Shell pollutes the drinking water. They suffer the most when, as in Brazil and Bolivia, the virgin forest is cleared to make way for farm animals and monocultures, and pesticides later contaminate water, food, and air. When fresh water is privatised by corporations like Nestlé and the groundwater level sinks.

Many Indigenous communities suffer from the psychological after-effects of their homes being destroyed, a condition known as »ecological grief«. Scientists who understand the consequences of ecocide experience the same trauma. One study found that the loss of the natural world had profound consequences for both Inuit people and Australian wheat farmers, leaving many with depression, despair, post-traumatic stress disorder, despondency, anger, and even suicidal thoughts. When a person realises how much of the natural world we've lost and are still losing, they often feel a deep pain, a pain that comes from having lost so many species, landscapes, and ecosystems that are fundamental to our way of life, our culture, and our traditions. It's also what we experience when certain landscapes disappear, for example, when glaciers thaw and are gone forever.

People who perceive all of this and are aware of their role in destruction of our habitat often feel guilty. This guilt occasionally can stop them from acting against environmental annihilation.

It's only natural that a process of this magnitude scars us psychologically, because we're both a part of nature and dependent on it. Four hundred years before Christ, ancient Greek philosophers such as Plato first conceived of nature as separate from humanity, and we've maintained this view ever since, taking nature apart and dividing it into elements. Many people, too many, immersed in the culture of our industrial societies, have forgotten to see human existence as closely tied to the natural environment. Only by feeling ecological grief can we reconnect with nature, and halt the destruction.

We've taken nature for granted for too long. In our outdated economic theories, nature wasn't even a factor; now, when it is considered, it is only as a resource, a commodity to use. In our economy-centred way of thinking, every inch is measured up in dollar signs – it's a philosophy that has even found its way into nature conservation.

You can see this pervasive financialization in concepts such as REDD+ (Reducing Emissions from Deforestation and Forest Degradation), a kind of modern selling of indulgences; forests are assigned monetary value, and if a forest is chopped down, the money is supposed to flow into projects that preserve another area of forest as a carbon sink in order to compensate for environmental destruction and emissions.

REDD+ has been widely criticised for not reducing emissions, and for treating different forests as ecologically interchangeable. Also, there's so much more to a forest than its perceived monetary value, especially for the people who live there and protect it best without needing incentives from international finance. But instead of recognising the role of Indigenous communities in environmental conservation, they're all too often driven out of their forests and deprived of their livelihoods. In other words, REDD+ leads to the violation of their human rights.

As long as we see nature as a commodity and use technocratic terminology to label the natural world, we can't break free of this destructive mindset. Abstract concepts detach us from the real natural world and allow us to dissect nature as a research object. Language shapes our thinking, so the way we talk about nature will be reflected in how we treat it, and vice versa. We should use words that make nature come alive, rather than just describing her functions or value as a commodity. Let's stop saying that we're depleting fish stocks and start saying that we're destroying shoals of herring. Let's stop talking about water resources and start talking about springs. Let's stop referring to aquatic biotopes and remember that they're marshes with reeds and wading birds.

Nature ensures the survival of our species. Biodiversity ensures that insects pollinate fruit blossoms and microorganisms purify water. It ensures that peatlands absorb carbon dioxide and that forests can withstand drought and invasive species. Nature doesn't just give us food to eat, water to drink, and air to breathe, she's a medicine cabinet, supporting our mental health and recreation.

However, the more that temperatures rise, and the more unstable that ecosystems become, animal and plant species increasingly die out. Species don't have time to evolve to changing conditions, and not all of them can migrate fast enough to avoid the heat. The less diversity there is on this planet, the less one species can easily be replaced by another with the same ecological function.

Invasive species – wasp spiders, *Hyalomma* ticks, grey squirrels, American red swamp crayfish – are conquering new habitats and upsetting existing ecosystems. Recently, the first mosquitoes were found on the Norwegian island of Spitsbergen. This hurts humans too, because invasive species can bring diseases to new places. The tiger mosquito, now found in parts of northern Europe, transmits formerly tropical diseases like dengue or chikungunya fever.

Ecosystems can withstand a lot of changes over a long time without collapsing. A missing stone doesn't cause a house to cave in. But we don't understand ecosystems well enough to know how many bricks we can lose before the building crashes.

In its 2019 report on species conservation, the World Biodiversity Council IPBES (Intergovernmental Science-Policy Platform on Biodiversity and Ecosystem Services) said that biodiversity is currently declining faster than ever before in human history. An estimated one million species are at risk of extinction. Five such mass extinctions have occurred before, but this time it's us humans who are responsible.

Instead of halting the loss of species and regenerating natural landscapes by rewetting bogs, removing river barriers, or reintroducing native species, we're continuing to saw off the branch we're sitting on.

The Earth system, our nature, has limits that we're constantly overshooting. We continue to live on credit, exploiting more than grows back.

Johan Rockström, who heads the Potsdam Institute for

Climate Impact Research, is working to determine the Earth's ecological boundaries, which, if crossed, will endanger humanity. In addition to climate change, these boundaries include ocean acidification, freshwater use, and biodiversity loss. Rockström warns that the disasters that would be caused by crossing these boundaries have not been properly recognised.

»The human burden on the global environment and ecosystems has reached a level where sudden systemic changes can no longer be ruled out,« he says.

The problem lies in our massive consumption of natural resources. Not because the world's population has grown, but because a small part of the population consumes too many resources; of the seven billion people on our planet, about 5 % use 25 % of the available resources and about 20 % consume 80 % of the energy.

The Global Footprint Network highlights how significantly these planetary boundaries are crossed by calculating what they call Earth Overshoot Day. Each year, overshoot day arrives earlier, and each country reaches it on a different date. In 2019, Qatar exceeded its share of resources on the 11th of February, Germany on the 3rd of May, while Indonesia didn't blow its annual budget until the 18th of December. While looking at our global »ecological footprint« can be instructive, the concept of the personal »ecological footprint« was promoted and spun by oil companies to shift responsibility onto consumers and away from producers.

If we protect intact landscapes and restore damaged ecosystems, humanity would stand a chance. We could even feed the world's entire population; there's enough food for all of us, we just need to distribute it better. People in industrialised countries who consume too much are not just robbing those living in poorer areas. They're also stealing from future generations.

According to experts, the climate crisis and ecosystem collapse are likely to have a dramatic impact on the world's population by the end of the century. According to the most extreme models, six billion people will die and just one billion could continue to live at the poles. Meanwhile, a study on food security calculated that food shortages could lead our civilisation to collapse by 2040. But such extreme scenarios don't have to happen, because we can change things.

The writer Jonathan Franzen recently published a piece in the *New Yorker* arguing that human psychology, political realities, and rising global energy consumption were making it near impossible for us to achieve the Paris goals. We should continue to make every effort, no matter how small, to reduce emissions, he says, but we also ought to face the truth and recognise that further action is needed as our societies destabilise due to food shortages and conflict. In light of the climate crisis, he insisted, everything we do collectively acquires new meaning, from fighting global injustice to defending fair elections. Putting an end to hatred on the internet once and for all, and pushing for fair immigration policies. Equality for minorities and all genders, civil order, a free press, the disarmament of the population – demanding and implementing all this has an impact on the climate. It's about creating a social system that is as strong and resilient as possible in order to be prepared for the difficult times ahead.

Franzen was heavily criticised for his stance; people said he'd given up and was sabotaging the potential for achieving the objectives of the Paris Agreement. But he's right in that we need to talk about adaptation as well as mitigation. In fact, adaptation is already necessary, and being implemented, in many countries of the Global South. But the opportunities for adaptation will shrink if we don't drastically reduce greenhouse gases now, which is why mitigation is more important in principle.

Nevertheless, it's high time to think about how we as humans want to adapt to global warming. If we want to limit it to 1.5 or 2 degrees Celsius, we need to decarbonise all sectors of society, including energy, mobility, housing, and agriculture. And, of course, we need the political will at all levels to implement this transition without shifting damage elsewhere. This will take time, even though it's clear that climate damages are increasing and conflicts may grow over the »scarce resources« that remain. Therefore, we must prepare our society and our social systems for this scenario, including standing up for democracy and promoting anti-racism in order to save lives at the EU's borders and to prevent autocratic or military takeovers.

In 2018, Professor Jem Bendell, who teaches at the Department of Sustainable Development at the University of Cumbria, published a monograph entitled »Deep Adaptation: A Guide to Lead Us Through Climate Catastrophe«, which questions the purpose of his entire discipline. In it, he explains how he concluded that the collapse of Western society is inevitable, catastrophe likely, and the extinction of humanity possible, and how this realisation led him to question his own work in the science of sustainability. Climate scientists have heavily criticised »Deep Adaptation«, stressing that Jem Bendell presents the current state of climate catastrophe as more dramatic and hopeless than it really is. Even more criticism has been levelled at the fact that the word »justice« is completely absent from Bendell's publication, and that he focuses mainly on Western society, instead of talking about those who have been affected by the exploitation and destruction of ecosystems for centuries.

Nevertheless, the text made me think about whether the current situation and the inaction of many political actors could mean the end of Western civilisation – or even of humanity itself. Whether it makes sense for us to continue our daily or professional lives in the middle of a dramatic ecological crisis. Every day that we fail to act, we endanger our survival as a species. We risk our food supply, our access to drinking water. Our infrastructure, our social lives. Our children's future.

Environmental degradation doesn't threaten our livelihoods equally. This is precisely where the great injustice lies. While some have the financial means to cope with rising food prices or to build mega dams to protect themselves from rising sea levels, others will have their family's survival threatened by rising grain prices, or by a single flood that destroys everything they own.

The destruction of our biosphere is running rampant. That's why rich states, who still believe they can externalise the consequences of their environmentally devastating lifestyles and economic systems by pursuing a rigid policy of isolation, must understand the extent to which life on Earth is under threat; because natural disasters can cause wars and could, possibly, even lead to the collapse of our civilisation. But politicians and the media present this to us in a far too innocuous manner.

The time has come to tell the truth about the climate crisis. About a crisis that is, in effect, only a symptom of our completely misguided understanding of our position as a species in the natural order. As long as we fail to put all our efforts into regenerating ecosystems and extending social justice, we have no future on this planet.

In our current system, politics and the economy cannot come to an effective solution. Electric vehicles, carbon taxes, emissions trading: they're neither sufficient nor efficient. This crisis can't be tackled with the same tools that caused it: the tools of neoliberal economic policy. As Albert Einstein said, we can't solve problems with the same mindset that created them.

Real change requires massive effort, but we have no choice.

We're in a crisis that threatens our very existence, and for the first time, the inhabitants of industrialised countries feel a little bit as threatened as those who have suffered colonisation and industrial exploitation for centuries.

To escape this trap, so that we can truly have a future, we have no choice but to radically change. Our generation faces a great challenge: to change the system that brought about this crisis.

As South African activist and environmentalist Kumi Naidoo, Secretary General of Amnesty International, says: »We need to be thinking not simply outside of the box; we have to take the whole box and throw it very, very far away.«

Chapter Four:
Questioning the System

The bright sunlight makes me blink as we leave the customs station. It's almost eight in the morning, but they're still not finished; now they have to check my details and take a photo for my file.

The police identification service is in the refugee camp. The island is so small, it only takes us a few minutes to get there. I just hope that when they've finished processing me, they'll take me straight to the place where I'm going to stay under house arrest until the hearing.

At the camp entrance, some of our passengers are sitting on the steps. When they see me, they applaud, and I stop to talk to them. So it was true, they finally got them off the boat.

I see the fatigue and concern in their faces. Their situation in the camp remains uncertain. It might be a long time before they know what will be done with them, whether any country will take them in. Just because they've made it to Europe doesn't mean they'll be allowed to stay. Maybe the entire gruelling journey, the agony at sea, was for nothing. The only consolation is that at least they made it out of Libya. I'm deep in thought when one of the officers who led me to the camp, a large, balding man, makes his way through the refugees, nods to me, and opens the glass door.

I climb the few steps and enter the low rise building. It's

almost as hot inside as out. A faint musty smell mixes with that of cleaning products.

The policeman leads me into a corridor lined with offices. It looks sterile, apart from a rubbish bin in the corner, full to the brim.

The officer opens one of the pale green doors. Mug shot, fingerprinting. The entire procedure is rather slow. When they finish, they take me back to the customs station to pick up my backpack (which someone from my crew has packed while we were at the identification centre), and then they take me to a whitewashed cottage. A woman is waiting at the entrance, and she immediately shows me to the room she prepared for me.

An hour later I'm showered and lying between clean sheets. Sunlight streams through the curtains, drawing a line on the wall, right in the middle of a photograph.

»Shit,« I think, »the mission's over and I can't go back to the ship. I promised the crew that we'd do a debrief of the whole mission together, but now they're going to have to do it without me.«

I feel like I'm breaking my word. But in my exhausted state, my eyes soon close and I fall asleep in an instant.

When I wake up, it's late in the afternoon.

I pass through a curtain of coloured beads and go out to the garden, where orchids and bougainvillea are in bloom. A small path marked with stones winds through potted palms and ends at an iron and glass table. At the table sits the woman who has taken me into her home.

A lizard basks in the sun on one of the stones. It darts away as I pass by.

My hostess is reading the newspaper.

She looks up and asks if I want coffee. The thought of another espresso turns my stomach; I had more than enough last night.

»I'd prefer a glass of water, thank you.«

She speaks very good English, which is useful; we'll be able to understand each other.

She tells me that someone from Sea-Watch gave her some food for me while I was in the shower. I'm not allowed to leave the house until the hearing, and in the meantime the only people who can visit me are my lawyers. I'm also not allowed to make phone calls or use the internet.

The middle-class rhythms of life in this house are a stark contrast to the camp. On Monday the police will pick me up at seven in the morning. The hearing will be held in Agrigento, capital of the province of the same name in southwestern Sicily, about four hours away.

On Sunday, of course, there's no statement saying what will happen to our former passengers; I fear we won't hear anything for weeks or even months. Although France, Germany, and Portugal have offered to take them in, it may be a long time before these promises are realised. There's nothing regulated about their resettlement; it's an opaque process, especially for the refugees themselves. They're in the headlines, but in the end, very few people actually care about their fate. The powerful send out tweets and the talk shows are being broadcast, but in the meantime, the real protagonists of this story are trapped in the camps, without access to information.

Public opinion, politicians, internet users, viewers – no one is looking where they should be.

Years ago, a tragedy occurred when an inflatable boat left

the Libyan capital of Tripoli for Lampedusa loaded with 72 people trying to reach the European mainland. That was in March 2011. In the middle of the sea, they ran out of fuel and drifted for a fortnight. Without food and water, left to fend for themselves, only nine people survived. But what makes this already tragic shipwreck even more terrible is that, according to the survivors, nobody answered the SOS they sent by satellite phone – even though ships of several nationalities came within sight of the boat. They described in detail an aircraft flying overhead, a military helicopter that dropped water and biscuits instead of rescuing them.

How does it feel to watch everyone with you die?

How does it feel when no one helps you; they just watch you suffer? Someone should have rescued these people and taken them to safety. Instead, most were left to die.

It's high time that everyone understands what the climate crisis and the collapse of our ecosystems are really about: survival. We must accept that we need immediate and effective action, which will inevitably involve somewhat drastic cuts for those living in the Global North. Yet these apparent cuts are in many ways not cuts at all. They will help people across the world – including ourselves – to live well.

We can choose to expand our humanity in the face of the climate crisis, or to let human rights deteriorate. We can choose whether to continue emitting huge amounts of greenhouse gases to boost our short-term interests, or to take effective action against the overexploitation of the planet.

The key, as climate activist and clinical psychiatrist Jane Morton says, is to talk about the crisis properly so that everybody understands the urgency of our situation. In her paper »Don't Mention the Emergency?« Morton explains that terms like »climate change« are far too innocuous, and allow people to avoid appropriate responses. We must stop talking about climate change and call it what it is: a climate catastrophe.

Only fear of collapse of the ecosystems, only concern for our own survival, will make us acknowledge the gravity of the situation and change our ways. From what I've seen on my polar journeys and in nature reserves, this fear is absolutely justified. It doesn't help to hide our worries or to try and play down the situation. It's too dangerous.

The climate emergency should always be in the headlines. We need more prominent voices telling the truth about the crisis, and we all need to talk about it more. Media coverage is quite uneven, and the danger of the situation we're facing has not been properly addressed by most outlets. How can we expect people to know what's going on if the media doesn't convey the urgency?

Jane Morton says that we shouldn't be talking about whether the Earth is warming by one or two or three degrees. The message must be that it's already too hot, and we don't want it to get any hotter. Many people in India and Bangladesh certainly see it that way.

We shouldn't talk about how many years we have left to act, or how big the remaining carbon budget is. That sort of talk allows us to push the issue further back, and sounds like there's some guarantee that 1.5 or two degrees is safe and that the global carbon budget (i. e. the maximum amount of carbon that we can emit) can be precisely calculated to keep us within that boundary.

This is all absurd. The carbon budget is an objective scientific measure, from which we can calculate the rate at which social change must happen. But if we only think in terms of these budgets, we won't act quickly. If we assume that we can cope with a certain level of heating, we'll postpone honest discussion of the climate catastrophe. Moreover, the policies of the Global North take this budget as a reference without accounting for the fact that many people are already affected by the climate catastrophe. People are already fleeing extreme weather and rising sea levels, because those responsible for these phenomena fall back on measures that allow for delay. The distribution of the carbon budget is a matter of fundamental fairness: a fair emissions reduction system would make rich nations reduce their budget faster than poor ones, so that poorer regions have time to determine how best to develop their infrastructure.

Instead of wasting time debating scientific facts with climate change deniers, we should concentrate on preventing disaster. When a house catches fire, you don't tell the occupants that you will consult on the measures that might need to be taken. You tell them clearly that they're in danger, evacuate them, and extinguish the flames.

Only when we understand how dangerous current developments already are for the inhabitants of the poorer countries and, very soon, will be for our own industrialised societies, will those who have been appeasing us start to take action. Then they'll want to do everything possible to prevent an average temperature rise of two degrees Celsius from taking us to the first tipping points in the climate system, and potentially catapulting us into a »heat age«.

It makes no sense to rely on organisations like NASA to find a habitable planet outside our solar system. They may think we should live on the moon, leaving the place where humanity arose; our home, a planet with a relatively temperate climate so far. Humans won't be able to inhabit the moon in the foreseeable future, and these technocratic solution myths provide no way out for our generation. The universe isn't going to lend us a helping hand. So we must mobilise all possible forces if we want to defend our rights against the politics of business as usual, against an economy focused on profit, competition, and growth.

Through her research, psychologist Renee Lertzman has found that most people refuse to accept the climate crisis, and that they deny it even to themselves, being caught between their desire to continue living as they are, and their aspiration to be part of the solution. To drive change, we're going to have to accept that it's normal to have mixed feelings about the climate catastrophe. We have to accept that it's normal to have complex emotions and we have to allow positive as well as negative thoughts: that the situation is serious and getting worse, or that we humans are an ingenious species, or that fixing the crisis will be difficult, or that the individual has a key role to play even though the general good is at stake. To find creative solutions and take effective action, we must communicate openly and address our fears.

We cope with the overwhelming loss of biodiversity in the same stages as we would when dealing with the loss of a loved one. First anger, then resignation, then denial, and, finally, acceptance. Some people are reluctant to mobilise against the climate crisis because they feel guilty for their own overconsumption. But to focus too much on the individual and their choices as a consumer only diverts attention from the real problem: that the system we live in is wrong.

The best time to change the system was at least half a century ago; the second-best time is now. Western society has known for nearly fifty years that our economic model and overconsumption are driving the world off a cliff. »The Limits to Growth«, the first Club of Rome report, was published in 1972. An interdisciplinary team led by scientist Donella Meadows analysed five global factors: industrialisation, population growth, malnutrition, exploitation of natural resources, and habitat destruction. This report stated that industrialisation, pollution, and population growth had such damaging effects that, together, they would devastate life on our planet in a hundred years.

If they were following the precautionary principle, politicians would have acted right there and then. Too much time has passed since that first Club of Rome report. In 1992 and 2004, the Club published two further reports which broadly confirmed the projections of »The Limits to Growth«. They warn that we're still devouring natural resources, and that our consumption of raw materials and the resulting waste cause significant harm to growing numbers of people worldwide, especially in the Global South.

With every warning published, many people certainly realised that we ought to put a stop to injustice and environmental destruction. The problem is that they don't yet feel directly affected. Thinking that change might lessen their standard of living, they don't want to change anything. Or maybe they just don't know where to start.

The Earth has more than enough resources to feed its seven billion inhabitants (and the ten billion expected in the future). Provided, of course, that it is mainly plant-based. The ethical issue is clear: we must weigh the perceived loss of eating less meat with the right to life of people who are threatened by the climate crisis.

Today we know that the problem isn't population growth per se, but the usage of resources and consumerism in rich countries. It has been said and proven ad nauseam: there are not too many people in the world. What there is, is a relatively small group of people that consumes too much. And the habits of this excessive minority exceed the planetary limits. To make matters worse, this group is expanding rapidly, as many countries are keen to copy this promising model of consumption and growth. To this we must add the interests of large multinational corporations who set the whole machinery in motion.

Still we put up with seeing the crisis intensify. Right now it's mostly people in poorer nations who are unfairly paying the price, but this will change, even if those of us in rich countries have more resources to protect ourselves from the consequences. For some time now, we've seen a trend of conflicts over resources, rather than solidarity in the face of catastrophe. We've seen countries closing their borders instead of saving people, and the political and social systems of many nations breaking down. The strategy our governments adopt to deal with these crises is one of violence. These conflicts are now in their infancy. But as the global climate worsens, they will escalate everywhere.

Syria was destabilised by drought, but the same is true of many other African nations. Clashes over farmland, such as those from 1981 to 1991 on the border of Mauritania and Senegal after a long drought, or the conflicts over the water of the Nile between Egypt, Sudan, and Ethiopia during the construction of the Grand Ethiopian Renaissance Dam, are likely to recur in the future with even more force. Let's not forget that the spark that ignited the first Arab Spring protests was food shortages, as the prices of cooking oil, sugar, and flour doubled and tripled.

All this worries the governments of richer countries, as they know that destabilisation helps terrorist groups like Boko Haram and the Islamic State to flourish. Former CIA director John Brennan admitted in a 2015 speech that he was concerned about security risks caused by food and water shortages; bear in mind it's generally the danger to their own countries that worries someone like Brennan most, not concern for the people directly affected.

These conflicts also lead to the spread of the disastrous model of growth. By financing one warring party or another, industrialised countries try to assert their economic and geopolitical interests. The moment a country becomes unstable due to political collapse or natural disaster, foreign companies have perfect conditions to move in and profit. Meanwhile the IMF and World Bank lay the foundations for future economic dependence by granting long-term loans, as writer and activist Naomi Klein demonstrated in »The Shock Doctrine«. Those profiting from this process are the local elites, who often sell land and public assets to foreign investors, acting against the interests of most of their compatriots – not to mention the economic system, which only has one objective: perpetual growth.

The concept of growth is deeply enshrined in the mindset of our societies. In the 1930s, US president Franklin D. Roosevelt promised to end the global economic crisis with his New Deal, a stimulus package of state-funded economic measures. It was geared towards one goal: economic growth. Since then, economic growth has become the measure of a nation's success. Subsequently, the war economy turned out to boost employment, productivity, and innovation, and with the »economic miracle« of the 1950s, rising prosperity – i.e. the availability of consumer goods to the entire population – became the driving force of the economy.

Since then, the main political objective has been to increase the monetary value of all goods and services of an economy, i.e. its gross domestic product (GDP). When growth slows down, conservative parties advocate the reduction of social services privatisation of public goods, austerity measures, and a return to traditional social models, because unpaid work within the family is often performed by women. Meanwhile, we keep on exploiting the environment, and people in poor countries work in miserable conditions to produce goods for the Global North.

The logic of economic growth – and politicians failing to acknowledge its downsides – is what led to this crisis of environmental destruction and human exploitation in the first place. It has resulted in a relentless pursuit of the wrong solutions. Companies strive for the highest possible profit, and social and ecological aspects are treated as secondary to financial returns. Competition puts companies under pressure, because in the globalised market only the companies that grow survive. To gain the upper hand over their competitors, they use advertising and marketing, which further drives the spiral of growth and consumption.

The competition paradigm also applies to relations between states – their own economies must be competitive, their own industries secure. This is clear in my native country, Germany, which is always striving to be the world's largest exporter. It's therefore not unusual for states to try and gain an edge over their competitors by subsidising fossil fuels, and encouraging consumption with incentives and subsidies instead of limiting energy consumption and resource use. We've even internalised the paradigm of growth and competition in our personal lives; we all want to be perfect, to have perfect children, and far too often see others as mere competitors. Even in our recreational activities we think we have to go »higher, faster and stronger«.

According to research by Climate Action Network Europe and other non-governmental organisations, the European Union spent over € 112 billion a year subsidising fossil fuels between 2014 and 2016, after having pledged to phase out subsidies to polluting companies by 2020. Most of these subsidies were tax exemptions for diesel, although they were also granted to coal, natural gas, and energy-intensive companies.

On top of that, the rich don't pay their taxes, and companies aren't held accountable for the environmental destruction they're causing. Everything is geared towards maintaining the system, so that those of us in industrialised countries can continue to live as we do and the economy can continue to grow. Anyone who thinks within the system can only think of crises as economic. They won't be able to think differently and advocate for a world in which what matters isn't competition, but finding our own meaning in life. If meaning were the focus of our system, not money, people would feel more able to cope with difficult situations on their own and be more involved in shaping society.

It's not surprising that, given the predominance of the growth imperative, the most important programme for dealing with today's crisis has taken the name of Roosevelt's economic plan – the »Green New Deal«. According to this plan, new, green, consumption would enable us to deal with the multiple economic, financial, and environmental crises. The Deal would create additional incentives to stimulate the economy. Green technologies and methods would create new jobs, and green investments would go into boosting renewable energy, public transport, and energy efficiency improvements for buildings. In this new green landscape, resources would be used sparingly, and eco-friendly innovations would create sustainable growth.

The underlying idea: to get our environmental problems under control, all we need is the proper technology. It's a naïve approach. It doesn't account for the fact that gains in efficiency are diminished, or at least massively reduced, by additional growth. There's no mention of the need for societal measures to enable us to live well with less consumption and production. The strategies offered by »green growth« are part of the system that triggered the crisis in the first place. Expanding renewables requires us to source more finite raw materials whose extraction is linked to serious ecological damage and human rights violations. Even »sustainable« products use natural resources and don't lead us to question whether meaning and contentedness aren't better achieved by means other than consumption. The supposed panacea of »green growth« doesn't question our perpetually hungry model of economic development.

Growth always goes hand in hand with the exploitation of resources and workers, and thus with damage to humans and the environment.

If, for example, electric vehicles are promoted as part of »green growth« (so as not to question the dogma of individual mobility), part of the car industry will grow as old cars are scrapped and new ones produced. Demand and subsidies thus ensure strong growth in one place, but it's short-term and comes with a price, i. e. the energy and resource-intensive production of electric cars. In this way, we reduce exhaust emissions in one place, while manufacturing causes emissions to rise elsewhere, mostly in other countries. Let's not forget the extraction of lithium, needed for vehicle batteries and also used in mobile phone batteries, which is found in the great Uyuni salt flats in Bolivia and in the border regions of Chile and Argentina. Its extraction generates a great deal of polluting dust and requires an enormous amount of water; around one million litres of the precious liquid are needed to obtain one tonne of lithium. In other words, electric vehicles are also resource-intensive and cannot be sustainably produced.

On top of that, the number of registered vehicles is increasing all the time, which is a problem in itself. Of course we need massive investments in non-fossil mobility. But to be truly sustainable, this must be paired with better public transport and infrastructure for cycling – as is only the case in very few countries. Furthermore, consumption must be reduced and fossil fuel-dependent industries phased out. The dilemma of »green growth« affects many industries. »Green growth« is based on the idea of using new technologies to avoid negative environmental impacts. The vision is to »decouple« economic growth from resource consumption: the economy continues to grow, but environmental damage grows more slowly – this is called »relative decoupling«. Another hope is that resource depletion will remain at the same level or decrease as the economy grows, but such »absolute decoupling«, studies show, is never the case.

The idea that decoupling alone can deal with the environmental crises we face is a pipe dream. Although the »carbon intensity« of the economy decreased by 0.6 % per year between 1990 and 2015, per capita income grew by 1.3 % each year, a 62 % increase in 25 years. Even if we support technologies that are supposed to decouple economic growth from resource consumption, the environment will continue to be negatively impacted by increasing economic growth.

Moreover, to avoid carbon emissions, we use problematic resources: in the case of electric vehicles, lithium ion batteries; in wind turbine magnets, rare metals like dysprosium and neodymium; in biogas or bioenergy plants, rapeseed and corn crops that need a lot of land to grow.

We're facing a structural problem.

So long as the amount of goods that we consume increases, natural resource consumption will inevitably grow. Three major studies have shown this in recent years. One, led by German researcher Monika Dittrich, calculated that with 2–3 % economic growth per year, even with efficient resource use, almost double the sustainable limit of resources would be consumed in 2050. Another study finds that, even if all countries were twice as efficient in resource use, and even with a global carbon tax of $ 236 per tonne, there would still be no reduction in resource consumption so long as economic growth is maintained. Finally, a study by the United Nations Environment Programme further tightened the screws in the equation. It shows that, even with a global carbon tax of $ 573 per tonne and government subsidies for faster efficiency increases, no improvement can be achieved – in fact more resources would be used, because the UN researchers were the first to consider that lower resource use makes goods cheaper, which in turn boosts demand.

Even under ideal laboratory conditions, »green growth« doesn't produce the results that policymakers hope for today. It is a dangerous economic illusion that will trigger further poverty.

Resource intensive industries are destroying the livelihoods of poor people in particular, through the appropriation of their land by corporations. A few rich people profit from being able to determine the prices of housing or water, and the poor can afford less and less due to inflation. This is happening in African countries, for example, many of which are theoretically rich because of their mineral resources, but where only a small minority of local elites and foreign investors actually gain from these minerals. To hide this injustice, statistics are altered by adjusting the measurement parameters depending on what the desired result is.

Before the World Bank had to raise the poverty line to $ 1.90 per day to meet the Sustainable Development Goals (SDGs), it was one dollar per day. The target for the United Nations Millennium Campaign at that time was to halve poverty worldwide by 2015. They achieved this goal ahead of time by embellishing the statistics and calculating the poverty of percentages of the population rather that the absolute numbers. A dollar a day for a person became income. Once population growth was factored in, poverty among the population shrank impressively on paper.

$ 1.90 a day doesn't consider the cost of living in varying countries. This poverty line is arbitrary and far too low – it would be more honest to start from a level closer to $ 7.40 a day, which allows people to purchase at least what science generally says is necessary for a reasonable diet and subsistence.

The real joke, however, is that wealth doesn't just promote poverty in other countries, it also doesn't usually make people happier after their basic needs are met. In fact, studies show that the pursuit of money and success runs counter to well-being and inner values. A life of prosperity, the life of an average European, comes at a high price; it's accelerated to warp speed by the media, mobility, and networking, among other things, and we often feel that our jobs are meaningless and that we work in highly dependent, hierarchical structures.

Another, far more serious problem is the unequal distribution of wealth and income. Even if GDP grows, wealth doesn't reach everyone equally, and while the richest 1 % of people own 40 % of the world's wealth, the poorer 50 % of the world owns only 1 %.

Studies show that equitable distribution benefits society: people are happier and healthier in societies where wealth is more equitably distributed, there is less violence, and less obesity. The system of perpetual growth, on the other hand, constantly drives us and creates inequality. It also leads to mental illness because we are supposed to push our capacities to the limit, and if possible, exceed them. If everything is supposed to grow all the time and we are constantly optimising ourselves, we'll never reach a goal, only stages in a breathless race. Almost everyone now knows someone who is affected by burnout, eating disorders, or depression – typical illnesses of our time often related to the philosophy of the achievement society.

We must introduce laws that curb resource consumption in affluent societies. Emissions trading is not the answer: it limits emissions, but by using market mechanisms that don't solve justice issues. It's a way to avoid a real solution by turning an ecological problem into a financial one. Above all, we need to set a limit on total resource consumption. Companies should not be allowed to profit from the destruction of nature. We have to stop exploiting other countries. To really improve things, climate conferences must stop focussing on »green growth«, and instead concentrate on reducing our consumption of resources, understanding in which areas growth is still necessary and where it is not, and discovering how we can live well in a system without economic growth.

A better economy would be oriented towards a good life for all. Its goal would be to avoid social injustice and poverty, and to make common goods – like the atmosphere, the polar regions, the oceans, space, and also the internet – available to everyone. Similarly, we must improve access to social goods, such as health care, education, affordable housing, and public transport. There must be clear rules for the use of these goods and a supervisory body that ensures that rules are observed and use is fair.

Many researchers are already thinking about what an alternative economic system could look like. Economist Kate Raworth has developed a model stating that the physical boundaries of our planet – such as overuse of water and land, climate change, destruction of the ozone layer, ocean acidification, and loss of biodiversity – must remain intact. At the same time, her model considers social needs that must be met, such as access to food and water, income and work, energy, education, and social equity.

Her economic system is shaped like a doughnut, with social needs making up the inner circle of the doughnut, and ecosystem boundaries comprising the outer ring. The inner foundations must not be met at the expense of destroying the outer environmental ceiling. A system that exceeds ecological limits just to grow, says Raworth, is of no use to us. We need a system that serves human beings, not one that only serves itself. A great deal of redistribution is necessary to create such a system, but it will ultimately lead to a more just and secure world in which neither the environment nor society are destroyed.

Anthropologist Susan Paulson, ecologist Giorgos Kallis, and many other researchers share the same opinion. The economy shouldn't be allowed to grow any further, because the current system increases social inequality, which not only affects the economy, but threatens the democratic foundations of society. They propose a system that rigorously rejects growth as the goal of the economy, which they call »degrowth«. There are many ideas in degrowth research:

- Eliminate GDP as an indicator of economic progress.
- Establish ecologically determined limits for carbon emissions and natural resource use.
- Introduce an additional carbon tax with revenues earmarked for social projects.
- Limit resource use and minimise waste.
- Agree on minimum and maximum incomes and establish a 20-hour working week.
- Taxation policy that reduces social inequality.
- Ban advertising.
- End subsidies and investments that cause environmental damage.
- Support the non-profit cooperative economic sector through subsidies, tax exemptions, and legislation.

This sort of post-growth economy is geared towards ecological sustainability and social justice, centring on human wellbeing. Post-growth means deceleration, time prosperity, and a new way of living together. Furthermore, the Global North must rapidly reduce its energy consumption to enable people in the Global South to shed neo-colonial dependencies, such as countries of the Global North making decisions about granting loans, or granting or denying debt relief. Only then can people in the Global South pursue a good life without copying the models of the North. Altogether, less energy and raw materials should be consumed.

Ideas of justice and new ways to define a good life are resonating in more and more places. In 2018, leading scientists and policymakers met in Brussels to discuss post-growth measures that could be implemented in Europe, and 238 degrowth scholars developed a set of proposals for EU action. In an open letter they called on the EU to establish a special commission on post-growth futures, and to evaluate economic strategies in terms of their impact on human wellbeing, resource use, inequality and sufficient income. The Stability and Growth Pact adopted by the EU should become a Stability and Wellbeing Pact, and every member state should have a Ministry for Economic Transformation.

We shouldn't focus exclusively on the negative effects of the crisis, or a potential unavoidability of events. There are many ways to avert disaster. We have reached a point in which our only option is to utilise the good ideas floating around.

Polluters must pay, and environmental destruction must be accounted for in our economic system. An unpolluted lake must be valuable in itself for our society, just as clean air and undamaged ecosystems must be considered an essential part of our life system.

Furthermore, we should abandon the GDP as a key measure and replace it with the Genuine Progress Indicator (GPI), which not only measures a country's production of goods, but also whether this actually translates into an increase in wellbeing. We urgently need a society and a political system in which our understanding of success and prosperity is not tied to our bank accounts, and where happiness is not based on the advertising industry's promises, but on genuine quality of life, wellbeing, and general satisfaction. Is the good life one that is based on individual profit, and ultimately on self-exploitation, consumption, and competition, when all this brings significant harm to people around the world? Or is it a life where the highest values are comprised of social contact, food safety, health, education, and pristine nature?

There are legal initiatives to create new legislation addressing the destruction of our planet, not to mention the lawsuits that have been filed on the subject. British lawyer Polly Higgins launched a citizens' initiative called »Make Ecocide Law« in which she takes legal action on behalf of nature. The initiative's aim is to ensure that ecocide, i. e. the destruction of nature via economic factors, is recognised as the »fifth crime« against humanity and peace, after genocide, war crimes, and other serious human rights crimes, so that it can be prosecuted. Then Shell could be sued for the climate crisis, BP for the oil spill in the Gulf of Mexico, and Tepco for the Fukushima nuclear disaster. Higgins called for prison sentences for the executives of major corporations who have caused ecocide.

Polly Higgins passed away in 2019, but the movement she spearheaded remains active, and its work highlights just how much current legislation is out of sync with the changing Earth system. She also demands changes in legislation to ensure that actions by corporations can be effectively punished. We could even go further and grant legal personhood to rivers, as has been done for the Ganges in India and the Whanganui in New Zealand, and we could even extend this to animals.

We urgently need governments willing to implement all this and allow greater participation in decision-making at all levels. We need real democracy in the economy, in politics, and in society. But democracy cannot be based on market laws alone. It must seek the benefit of all based on development, support, and environmental protection, and eliminate anything that conflicts with these goals.

This is an unprecedented challenge, and we need all democratically minded people to meet it. We only have two options: we can either throw our planet's ecosystems off balance – which simply isn't a solution! – or we push for a global transformation, a radical reorientation of our system that will fundamentally reshape society. And by this, I mean: if we succeed and someone were to time-travel a hundred years into the future, they would encounter a radically different system.

For such a transformation to be beneficial for all, we need to make the democratic process more inclusive – we would have to form a living democratic community together. Because the problem isn't democracy itself, but the fact that right now, it isn't acting in the interest of all, or the interest of the next generation. It serves the economy. This needs to be changed.

Kurt Tucholsky is credited with saying, »If elections really changed anything they would be banned«. Today many people, convinced their vote is worthless, fail to go to the polls. This apathy is clearly due to the fact that career politicians are unwilling to give up their power – and that in every election period, they clearly act in favour of the lobby and against the interest of their voters.

This is one of the reasons why elections are dangerously changing today's reality; they are destabilising democracy. The World Values Survey (WVS) found that, of 73,000 people surveyed in 57 countries, 92 % considered democracy to be the right system of government. However, the desire for a »strongman« leader has also increased over the past decade. The loss of trust in politics is already visible in governments that have been barely able to form majorities for years, such as Spain, Belgium, and Austria, and in my country, Germany, the far-right party *Alternative für Deutschland* (AfD) has gained so many seats in state parliaments that it is getting difficult to form coalitions against them. According to the WVS, only 30 % of voters have confidence in their national parliament.

Voting alone is not enough. In a world that is constantly changing, we only have elections every four years. For four years, we're condemned to inactivity in the current system, because we're not making use of our democracy's full range of possibilities. In a good democracy, power comes from the people; but for that to happen, the people must participate. In order to work, democracy must be lived. But not through simple referendums where we can only vote yes or no.

Politics is a complex matter – we need real participation and active social movements. Citizens must be involved in decision-making, because parliaments are paralysed and politics is out of touch with urban and rural realities. Instead, it's focused on businesses, which invest a lot of money to sway policy-makers. Many of the political decisions in recent decades were clearly lobby-driven. According to Lobby Control, an independent NGO, around 25,000 lobbyists influence EU policies, backed by an annual budget of € 1.5 billion.

It's a bad system, far too dependent on lobbyists and far too determined by career politicians seeking re-election. We need to reinvent democracy by learning from the democratic systems of the past: elections are not the only way citizens of a democracy can participate in decision-making. To adequately represent people's interests, democracy must be deliberative; this includes public debates at the municipal level, and citizens' assemblies comprised of randomly chosen participants.

The NGO »Mehr Demokratie« (More Democracy) has already made a start in Germany, setting up a citizens' council to develop policy proposals in a process modelled on the Irish Citizens' Assembly. Following various regional conferences, an assembly is held with randomly selected citizens who develop a report containing concrete proposals for improving democratic processes. Various experiments have shown that such randomly selected citizens' assemblies produce surprisingly well-founded decisions and good policy proposals.

The clearer we define the way of life we want to adopt, the less exhausting the challenges will seem. It's all about the narrative, the Big Story. We must start telling a better story about the future we want to achieve. So far we've been told that a zero-carbon future is difficult to achieve. That changing our way of life is avoidable as long as we pass a few reforms. Or we've been told a story that casts our struggle to curb climate change as a fight against a faceless opponent who is stronger than us anyway.

We need to understand that things can be better after this transformation. That the economic system we live in harms us anyway, that it fosters inequality and poverty. That there's a relatively small group of global elites who benefit handsomely while billions of people suffer and are robbed of opportunity. That we can bring about change together.

That, in the long term, we'll all benefit from a more equal society. That we can have car-free city centres, better air, food produced without animal torture or pesticides. Goods that aren't produced in a system of modern slavery. Healthy nature to which we feel attached because we know we can't live without it. A life in harmony with our values.

We must talk about what sort of society we could be. We need to paint a picture of a future that is worthwhile and so beautiful that many other people will want to be part of it and will work towards it. Only then will perceived loss turn into gain.

Unlike the fairy tale that anyone can make it in this society if they work hard, and that our economic system is about prosperity for all, this is actually the truth.

The climate crisis is a collective, all-encompassing problem. The only way to tackle it is to stop working against each other, because we can only succeed if we cooperate. Collaboration is what made our species so efficient as we evolved. We all have to work together to pressure governments to end their idleness, and to develop solutions for the future.

We can counter the crisis with protest and creativity. We have to transform every part of our existence; not just the structure of our states, but our very way of life. Above all, because we need to make good things happen quickly in this critical phase, we need a new culture of engagement and protest. Or to use my own example: we can't wait for them to let us into a harbour and then treat people as they please. We need to disrupt the current order and create possibilities for a more just world.

We must join forces.

There must be many of us.

We aren't yet a majority. But it's not just the climate system that has its tipping points – there are social tipping points too. New things always take time to establish themselves. They start with some people who are ahead of the curve and formulate demands; once they gain enough support and the protest becomes visible enough, these new ideas spill into the mainstream. Today we've reached a point in which many people find it strange to continue thinking and acting as we have up to now. Even if that was normal before.

The more movements like Extinction Rebellion and Fridays for Future there are in the world, the more visible the protests will be, and the more important they will become. The better the media report about these groups and events, the more common it will become to participate in them, until one day it'll be strange not to be part of a protest movement.

Many are still intimidated by the consequences and the inconvenience of getting involved. But inaction will have dire consequences for everyone.

We're entering a period of consequences, Winston Churchill once declared.

Today, we've entered one again.

Chapter Five:
Let's get cracking

A swarm of journalists and news vans is waiting for me as we drive up to the entrance to the Agrigento court-house, a functional building with a glass façade on whose portico is written the word »*Iustitia*«-justice. To avoid the media hullabaloo, we enter directly through the garage. I don't appreciate the media paying so much attention to me, when they're denying it to the real protagonists: the people rescued by *Sea-Watch 3*. We walk to the courtroom where my case is being tried, the soles of my shoes squeaking on the stone floor. After briefly conferring with my lawyers, we take our seats opposite the judge. She is in the gallery, seated at a simple table, and it is she who has the power to decide on the legality of my detention.

She looks at her file for a moment, then nods to the sworn translator, who is sitting at a separate table, between the Prosecutor's desk and ours. Then we start to reconstruct our entire rescue operation right up to the moment we entered the harbour. The evidence presented is reviewed, discussed point by point, translated, and recorded in the minutes. The judge wants to know everything in detail – why Libya and Tunisia are not safe havens, and how the European authorities have not responded to the information provided by our organisation.

Even though my Italian is very rudimentary, it's obvious to me that the translator has misrepresented some of the things I've said in English. This sort of thing happens occasionally in court, so we came with our own translator. Luckily the judge seems to understand me anyway, and she ends up correcting the translator herself.

She will pass sentence tomorrow evening, and in the meantime, I remain under house arrest.

»We won!« my lawyer exclaims enthusiastically when he calls me the next day, sometime after nine in the evening. And in some ways, we've also achieved much more.

It was clear that I was most likely going to be released even before the judge delivered her verdict, because the Public Prosecutor's Office had only asked for my expulsion from the province of Agrigento. But what I didn't expect was that the judge would make such a clear statement on the situation that had brought me before her: although she was only supposed to determine whether my detention was justified or not, she pointed out that Libya and Tunisia could not be considered safe havens, and also that our entry into the port of Lampedusa was justified because of the emergency situation.

Still, the Public Prosecutor's Office will continue to investigate, and when it's finished, in a year or two, I could find myself being charged with illegal entry into the port or inciting illegal immigration.

But even if I'm tried or convicted: given the chance, I'd do it again.

It doesn't matter what penalties or punishments they throw at me. Compared to what all these people are going through, my punishment is nothing. That's why I find it intolerable that one thing again was not on the agenda: the crisis of human rights that we're in the midst of.

I thought a lot about how I could let the refugees themselves have their say in this book. In the end, I felt that it would not do justice to the people with their very individual biographies if snapshots of them were included here, so to speak, as if there were nothing to say about them apart from their brief stay on the *Sea-Watch 3*. So I've refrained from doing that. I demand that the people who are most affected by this – no, by any rescue mission – be asked directly. They don't need me to be the transmitter of their stories. Nor is their story that they were guests on the *Sea-Watch 3* for 17 days. Once the state of uncertainty and the many mountains of paperwork caused by the European asylum system are behind them, the people themselves will perhaps want to tell the stories of how they experienced their flight, as well as their backgrounds, and what came after.

If we want to transform our society, we need to listen to each other. It's important to open ourselves to other cultural perspectives, because to live together well on this planet, we need to understand each other.

While my appearance before the judge was proceeding relatively quickly, the people we saved with the *Sea-Watch 3* were still stranded in Italy. They were registered as refugees in Italy, even though several other countries and more than 60 German cities had said a day before our arrival in Lampedusa that they were willing to take them in.

Days go by and nothing happens. In the weeks that follow, these people who have fled oppression and economic hardship, political conflict and lawlessness in Eritrea, Nigeria and Somalia, in Cameroon, Côte d'Ivoire and Libya, primarily do one thing: wait.

They have to be interviewed by the European Asylum Support Office. They must give detailed answers to the representatives of each of the states willing to receive them. France interviewed twelve, but only accepted nine. We don't know why three had to stay in Italy; the criteria each country uses to decide who they'll take in aren't transparent. Almost all those rescued were taken to a reception centre in the Sicilian town of Messina, where they were held in an internment camp, with the entrance guarded by the police. It was only when lawyers intervened that they were granted freedom of movement beyond their curfew, a right that remained refused to all other detainees. Medical care is scarce and psychological help practically non-existent. Gradually, they are dispersed far and wide; some go as far as Portugal, Finland, or Luxembourg, others stay temporarily in Italy.

This process must be unbearably hard for someone who has suffered so much to reach Europe. As environmental activist and human rights lawyer Hindou Oumarou Ibrahim notes in the foreword:

»No one should be forced to leave their home, to risk their life, just because there is no future for them in their native land. No one is happy to leave their family, their roots, their identity. We should never forget that no one is born a migrant. So, we must stand and say clearly that we don't want this future. Then, we have to make changes.«

We can't stand idly by any longer, because the window of opportunity to stop the ecological crisis is closing. Our backs are against the wall.

When we were on *Sea-Watch 3*, we didn't have much

choice either; that's exactly why we decided to act. In the end, I had given up hope that the authorities – the Coast Guard, political representatives, the Public Prosecutor's Office – would take action. References to the legal situation were ignored, medical reports fell on deaf ears. All the calls to authorised representatives, all the emails we sent, were in vain. But the moment I realised that no one else was going to provide us with a way out was the moment in which I found my own solution.

It's a similar situation with environmental and climate sciences, which continually provide us with a kind of medical report on the state of the Earth.

The diagnosis is life-threatening.

But because we've waited too long for someone else to solve the problem for us, we cannot postpone any longer. Human beings are suffering, ecosystems are suffering; many of the changes triggered across the globe are already irreversible, and some species are already lost forever.

No one in politics is offering up a solution.

We need to act.

We, as civil society.

And that's why I'm turning to *you*, dear reader. If you've read these pages, then you know full well that we're faced with a catastrophic situation. You know enough about the crisis. You know that the time has come for all of us to do something about it.

Obviously, you can carry on as if nothing were happening. Carry on with business as usual. Watch governments fail to take sufficient action on climate change. You can live your life, finish your studies, go to work in a bank, start studying economics, buy furniture for your new home, plan your next trip. But remember that everything, absolutely everything you do, affects the climate, even when you decide to do nothing about it. Especially then, because that's a decision that leads us all into the abyss.

But there's another choice. You can also be part of the change. You can help us find a way to shape our future ourselves before someone else does it for us.

Together we can build a democratic society that doesn't slavishly worship money, growth, and relentless consumption. A society committed to solidarity, justice, and community. A society in which prosperity means simply that we all do well.

Our time on earth is very limited, so why not do something meaningful with it? We can save lives. Or we can let the crisis happen right under our noses, putting the lives of countless people at risk.

What do you choose?

We've reached a crucial moment in history, possibly the last years in which we can still avoid overshooting the boundaries that can keep us from entering a global heat age.

If you're part of the generation that will be exposed to climate collapse in full force, now is the time to stand up for your future.

If you're older, now is the time to do something for our future generations.

Whatever generation you belong to, what matters is that this is the time for global justice, because by acting on the climate crisis you're standing in solidarity with the people who suffer its impacts.

This is the moment when all generations are beginning

to realise that the political system is failing. When we stop listening to the greenwashed promises of corporations.

Those of us who stop hoping that they'll be able to solve our problems will realise that we're the ones who have to act. And everyone who can act has the obligation to do so – especially those of us living in relatively prosperous countries where we're able to rely on the rule of law; a privilege in today's world. People in industrialised countries have far more power and opportunities to stand up for human rights and oppose destructive economic and political practices than someone living in the Sahel or other regions in crisis, who can't even meet their basic needs.

We have to act. »Right here, right now, is where we draw the line,« raged young Swedish activist Greta Thunberg in her speech at the 2019 Climate Summit. »The world is waking up and change is coming, whether you like it or not.«

It's up to us to take Greta at her word and draw that line of truth. It's up to us to ensure that her speech doesn't just hit the headlines once and then fade into obscurity, as happened to the words of then-twelve-year-old Severn Cullis-Suzuki, who at the Rio Summit back in 1992 insisted that we cannot go on like this. With the not-insignificant power that we have as citizens of wealthy states, we can stand up for that which Severn and many Indigenous activists around the world have been repeating for a long time, and which Greta just reiterated.

If you're angered by political inaction, good, because your anger at the current system is our greatest opportunity. The vast majority of movements, of social change, are not based on hope, but on angry people with their backs to the wall. Only out of anger and hopelessness comes the realisation that if you do something, the consequences of the crisis will be less dramatic than if you do nothing.

That is when courage grows. Recalling Gandhi's salt march in 1930, the massacre of young black demonstrators in Soweto in 1976, or the peaceful revolution in East Germany in 1989, we can see that all these movements have one thing in common: the people that made up these movements were deprived of some fundamental right, and they had a solution that they were determined to achieve. The solution I see – the thing I absolutely believe must happen – is for us to take action, whether it's by rescuing shipwrecked people in the Mediterranean or stopping environmental collapse. They're simply two sides of the same coin, different symptoms pointing to the same systemic problem. I'm disappointed in those who have let this crisis happen through their inaction, I'm afraid of what will happen if I do nothing, and I'm confident that things will improve if I get involved. Those of us who give up hope start looking for their own solutions.

One of the first actions staged by German Greenpeace activists in October 1980 was to chain themselves and their lifeboats to a ship loaded with toxic waste, the *Kronos*, to prevent it from dumping its hazardous cargo in the North Sea: they were fed up with this scandalous environmental practice.

Despite unequal power relations, some of the many protests by Indigenous peoples have been successful if they've managed to last long enough. The Dondria tribe, an Indigenous community living in Odisha, in eastern India, has been protesting for years against the company Vedanta Resources that wants to build a bauxite mine on their land.

The dust from the mining, the exhaust fumes and oil from the machines, as well as the toxin-laden sludge, would have destroyed the nature they depend on. They have organised many, many protests, with non-violent actions like blocking the roads and chaining themselves to the site; and with the help of a media campaign, they have finally got what they wanted (at least in part). For the time being, there will be no mine on their territory. It's David's victory over Goliath.

Protests like this are happening all over the world, even in industrialised countries. They remind me of the years of resistance in the Hambacher forest in western Germany. The company RWE planned to dig up the forest for an opencast coal mine, but by erecting huts and treehouses, protesters managed to stall the project. Activists in the area, together with other groups such as those for people displaced by coal mining, have succeeded in keeping RWE in the news and in saving part of the forest area.

Somewhat less dramatically, the citizens' movement for new energy hasn't waited for Europe to change the way it produces electricity: citizens have simply banded together, and are building wind power plants and putting up solar panels themselves. They're tackling the energy transition on their own. This is how community action brings about change.

All you need is a goal – and a good plan.

The time to act is now. Every step, no matter how small, counts. We can't afford to give up just because we think we're not going to achieve enough. In the face of rapidly advancing climate change, any attempt to maintain ecosystems, however futile it may seem, is important. But it's not enough to protect what already exists; we've already lost too much. We need to regenerate and re-naturalise vast stretches of our environment; to reintroduce native species and restore forests, wetlands and grasslands as closely to their original state as possible.

Plus we need to think as far ahead as possible. When I was in Scotland transplanting native trees, I realised how controversial even this action can be. We were trying to conserve something that can't be maintained, because human activities are impacting ecosystems at such an alarming rate. To know which trees you plant will be flourishing 100 or 300 years from now, you'd have to be a fortune teller. No one knows which tree species are certain to grow in a given region as the climate changes, or which ones will be able to cope with the invasive species that may be present in a hundred years' time. Only one thing is known for sure: we need to focus on mixed forests, not monocultures, because having a range of species will hopefully ensure that at least a few will be able to adapt to the climatic conditions of the future.

The time to act is now. First and foremost, we must tell the truth, and call the crisis affecting the existence of our Western civilisation by its real name. We have to stop arguing about the facts – we've amassed more than enough scientific data on the climate crisis and the collapse of our ecosystems. People who want to continue using fossil fuels to satisfy their economic interests like to turn it into an opinion poll and cast doubt on proven facts. What we need is to accept these inconvenient truths and make realistic plans for how to deal with them.

For example, some scientific studies say that we urgently need to change our food production systems, and therefore our diet. For the first time, these studies consider not only the emissions generated by land use, but also the volume of carbon sinks that are lost in cultivated soils and land that is used exclusively for the production of feed for livestock. If the land were freed from overuse, these areas could be re-naturalised and protected. This is a much more feasible way of extracting greenhouse gases from the air than through other technology-based proposals which are not yet available and whose benefits are uncertain, to say the least.

The Green Belt Movement led by scientist Wangari Maathai, who advocated reforestation in Kenya focussing on the needs of local people, proves that such reforestation strategies are perfectly feasible. It's precisely these kinds of projects that initiatives such as Natural Climate Solutions are calling for: projects that regenerate ecosystems that capture and store carbon, such as swamps and marshes, mangroves, wetlands, and forests. Of course, we also need to stop destroying ecosystems and pumping out greenhouse gases, and natural climate solutions can't be used for greenwashing or as an excuse to keep burning fossil fuels. We need to invest much more in these solutions, as only 2.5 % of subsidies go to carbon capture efforts. However, this whole process will entail major changes in our way of life; animal farming for human consumption will have to be limited to a considerable extent. Many will find this an inconvenient truth, but we won't succeed in protecting our ecosystems unless we accept it.

The time to act is now. Civil society movements have always been the driving force for change. The bigger they get, the more likely they are to achieve their demands.

There's no denying that it's good to limit personal consumption, i. e. not to buy too many new clothes, not to travel by plane, and not to eat meat. But that's not enough. The ecological crisis is a structural, systemic, and global problem that can't be solved by personal changes alone. If you're conscious of the seriousness of the situation, of course you feel obliged to cut your contribution to the problem – but individual measures must be accompanied by community actions and political initiatives that work towards system change.

Every movement starts small, usually with a handful of supporters. According to research by political scientist Erica Chenoweth, for a protest movement to be successful, only 3.5 % of the population needs to participate in a committed manner. In New Zealand, this many people have already participated in climate strikes; but it would take their sustained commitment to drive change. While political party membership is declining across Europe, citizens' movements are on the rise around the world. We're facing problems that need to be understood as an existential crisis that cannot be dealt with based on political affiliation. More and more people are realising that we need to mobilise against climate change. The Fridays for Future protests have shown that the call to combat climate change is resounding around the world. If this momentum grows stronger, it is all of us, the members of the »last generation« – the people who will be alive to shape the crucial decades ahead – who can do most for the preservation of human society.

The time to act is now. In order to win, we have to look at how other social and political movements have succeeded in the past. Social science can show us how a protest movement is built and what forms of action actually work, i. e. what we need to do to be effective. We must act here and now, because we're on the verge of the climate tipping points. The climate crisis is, above all, a question of global justice. We can prevent the suffering of so many people if we take the right steps.

Political scientist Erica Chenoweth studied the success and failure of more than 300 social movements, based on whether or not they remained non-violent. To her surprise, she found that non-violent protests were twice as likely to succeed as violent ones. According to her study, non-violent movements are much more inclusive, i. e. they include people from a wide range of age groups and social groups who cannot or do not want to support violent protests. Inclusion is essential for success; only then do movements reach the critical mass needed to bring about profound change. Non-violence also presents repressive regimes with a moral dilemma that can only work to their disadvantage, also called the »paradox of repression« or »backfiring«. They must stifle the movement to maintain the status quo, but as soon as they resort to violence to suppress peaceful protesters, public outrage draws more people into the movement.

However, it's often difficult to judge whether a particular movement or revolution was completely non-violent. Often, alongside a fundamentally non-violent movement, there was a »radical wing« that engaged in sabotage, destruction of property, and sometimes even violence against people. These radical wings were sometimes in conflict with the peaceful majority of the movement. Looking back, it can be hard to pinpoint the moment a »radical wing« became so dominant that it succeeded in marginalising the movement's initial principle of non-violence. Sometimes it's the case that militant radical wings that emerge within or alongside a peaceful movement are ignored or forgotten, distorting its history. Iran's »peaceful« revolution of 1979 involved some armed street fighting in Tehran, for instance, and the People Power Movement may not have succeeded in overthrowing the Philippine dictatorship of Ferdinand Marcos in 1986 without the militant Communist movement and the Muslim Freedom Movement. Likewise, the US government's concern that people frustrated by years of failure in the civil rights movement would eventually join more militant – rather than non-violent – groups provided Martin Luther King with crucial leverage. We should also recognize that colonised peoples were only able to liberate themselves from slavery and oppression by using violence, as Frantz Fanon lays out in »The Wretched of the Earth«. But today, environmental or anti-racist movements face a different situation. Also, the First Nations who – as *water protectors* – protest against pipelines and demand rights to their lands in North America are not calling for violent resistance. According to researcher Sakshi Aravind, their centuries-old struggle against the violence and dispossession of settler colonialism is based on strategic pacifism. Still, isolated activist groups have sabotaged pipelines – without harming people – insisting that burning fossil fuels itself is already a form of extreme violence.

Nevertheless, we should be aware that the time following the upheaval will carry on the structure of our movements.

This means we have to ensure that our movements reflect the more just future we're striving for, and they need to reflect it today, which is why they need to be inclusive, democratic, anti-racist, and aim to dismantle power structures which keep injustices in place. Therefore, non-violence against people is absolutely essential. All this requires discipline and organisation, but it allows us to gain support across all segments of society, and it's both ethically and strategically crucial, as otherwise the movement might split, whether as a result of internal frictions or external backlash, and consequently be weakened politically. Still, we shouldn't forget that violence is already being used – often by state actors – mainly against people of colour, for example through the EU's migration policy or massive greenhouse gas emissions.

The time to act is now. Our resistance movement can only succeed if we plan well. I used to think that conventional political work, such as that carried out by governments and environmental NGOs, was the right path to take. But it hasn't been effective: despite all the good intentions, greenhouse gas emissions have increased by 60 % in the last 30 years, and ever more species of wildlife are in danger of extinction.

Journalist Mark Engler and his brother Paul, a lawyer specialising in labour law, explain in their book »This is an Uprising« that peaceful movements must have a well-thought-out strategy to succeed. By analysing the momentum generated by successful protest movements, they defined the best way to build a successful movement. They discovered that the insights into leadership organisation taught at universities, for instance by Marshall Ganz at

Harvard, can also make protest movements successful: they have an overarching narrative, a strategy, and a structure that are embedded in the movement's DNA, and they're reflected in many of their tactics and actions.

The clearer the objective of the movement is, the less time it will take to reach a critical mass. Everything must be geared towards achieving its goal, but that goal must also be far reaching: the Arab Spring, i. e. the protests, uprisings, and revolutions in the Arab world between 2010 and 2013, ended in failure because oppressive regimes were overthrown but nothing new was built. Movements that emerge quickly and then lose momentum are generally too dynamic to engage in the structured processes necessary to consolidate success. Even if a movement is able to achieve prompt political change, it must also have a strategic plan for what comes next, and for that, it needs structure, organisation, and cooperation with existing civil society structures.

One of the successful movements that Mark and Paul Engler analyse in their book is the Serbian grassroots movement Otpor! (»Resistance!«). In 2000, this movement launched a political campaign supporting opposition parties to join forces against dictator Slobodan Miloševic and bring democracy to the country. Having achieved this goal, Otpor! founded a non-profit organisation in Belgrade called the Centre for Nonviolent Action and Strategy, which disseminates Otpor!'s own tactics and experiences along with other teachings on non-violent resistance.

According to Srđa Popović, co-founder of Otpor!, it's important for the movement to have a clear strategy and an unmistakable appearance. It should, for example, have an easily recognisable symbol and a clear goal, but there also has to be enthusiasm and, of course, humour, a fundamental tool of any protest movement that allows us to laugh at those in power. And, of course, presence. It's no use, says Popović, just being active on the internet; even the Arab Spring wasn't a phenomenon that evolved exclusively on Twitter. Tweeting just sped up communication. There's nothing more effective than people on the streets taking risks to defend their rights and freedom.

The time to act is now. To bring about rapid change, there must be mass mobilisations and as much disruption of public order as possible, because that eventually leads to public discussions and resolutions.

The protests of the suffragettes in the early twentieth century are a good example of effective mass protest movements. Emmeline Pankhurst, the women's rights activist and founder of the Women's Social and Political Union (WSPU), developed a theory of resistance to achieve the movement's goals non-violently – but from the very beginning, this included things like smashing shop windows in the city centre. Just three years after the founding of the WSPU, the movement counted 260,000 supporters. The suffragettes petitioned the Prime Minister, disrupted election rallies, made public speeches, organised large demonstrations, demanded entry to the House of Commons, and repeatedly got themselves arrested. Their actions escalated from founding a women's parliament, to a hunger strike in prison, to refusing to take the census, to founding a women's party. Emmeline Pankhurst, however, turned increasingly violent over time and advocated the use of explosives, which led to several prominent members and two of Emmeline's daughters leaving the WSPU in 1913 in dispute. After 15 years and the ongoing protests of thousands and thousands of women, the first – still unequal – right to vote for women was introduced in Britain. Years later, political scientist Gene Sharp explored the many possibilities of civil resistance. His book »From Dictatorship to Democracy« was read by people who supported the civil protests in East Germany, Burma, and Egypt. His 198 methods of non-violent action are collected on a website, under Sharp's three main headings: methods of non-violent protest and persuasion, such as speeches, books and mass petitions; methods of non-violent social, political, and economic cooperation, such as student strikes, consumer product boycotts, or a tenants' strike; and finally, methods of non-violent intervention, such as sit-ins, occupations, or whistleblowing.

My entry into the port of Lampedusa caused a stir in the media, and a dilemma: here was a person being punished for defending human rights, while, on the other hand, our governments were violating those same rights.

Let's disrupt the governments who only care about constant growth and staying rich. Let's disrupt the power companies that are cutting down healthy forests and destroying the land to extract coal, that – in light of rising temperatures – we shouldn't burn anyway. Let's disrupt the industry and companies that have been stalling the fossil fuel phaseout for decades with their lobbying and falsified studies, and those that manufacture in other countries under inhumane conditions to save costs. By letting these people have their way, we're accepting that the people in power are doing nothing – or not enough – to counter the climate crisis and the destruction of nature. We're allowing companies to put profit before the well-being of the majority. And we're specifically tolerating the fact that people are drowning in the Mediterranean or suffering violence from the far right on the streets. Let's disrupt – but for the right reasons.

The time to act is now. For protests to be successful, they must be able to uphold their momentum. We know from the trade unions that a labour strike isn't effective if it only lasts a day. It needs to last as long as necessary to achieve the overarching goal; it has to disrupt the normal production process; and it has to cost the company money. It can also target an institution's public image.

Roger Hallam, who became known as one of the 15 co-founders of Extinction Rebellion, but who later caused a lot of damage to this movement and was asked to leave it, demonstrated that sometimes the actions of just one person can be enough. When he was a PhD student at King's College London, Hallam showed his disapproval of his university's investment in fossil fuels by spraying washable chalk on the walls of the central auditorium. As punishment, he was expelled, barred from entering the building, and prosecuted. None of this stopped him: Hallam went on hunger strike for two weeks. Five weeks later he succeeded in getting the university to commit to phasing out its investments in fossil fuels by 2021 – a win which came about because Hallam was more persistent than other students who had tried before him but perhaps could not or did not want to risk being expelled.

The time to act is now – wherever we can make the biggest splash. Mass action should focus on the capital, because that's where the centre of power is and that's where you're sure to get the media's attention. It's rather unusual for the world press to send their correspondents to the provinces, as happened with *Sea-Watch 3*.

The time to act is now. It's worth bearing in mind that a protest movement must continually grow and mobilise more supporters. As the number of people supporting Martin Luther King and Mahatma Gandhi grew, so did the chances of success of their respective movements. The stories we tell make it seem as though King and Gandhi were the only heroes, the ones who single-handedly pushed for change, when in fact they did so backed by thousands upon thousands of supporters. If a social movement wants to achieve its goal and not weaken along the way, it must strive to always convey what its core elements are, the premises on which its action is based, and its tactics (its DNA, one might say). Otherwise, disagreement over tactics or core principles may arise and stall the movement or bring it to an end completely. Disagreement over tactics can seriously harm an entire activist organisation. This was the case in Extinction Rebellion UK, when a few members of the movement blocked the underground in a working-class area during rush hour while most of the activists on that day participated in an occupation against the arms trade. Those blocking public transport knowingly acted against the wishes of the others, and drew criticism towards the whole movement.

The time to act is now. Our protests must be fun and full of life. They have to awaken a person's natural creativity, and offer something radically new. We can learn from Banksy's street paintings, which appear overnight, always in new locations. We can learn from the posters and costumes at rallies: The more creative and funny they are, the more likely they are to be seen in the media, and therefore the more likely the message of the protest will spread. In Germany, an art collective called the Centre for Political Beauty (*Zentrum für politische Schönheit*) built a miniature replica of the Berlin Holocaust Memorial in front of the private residence of a well-known right-wing extremist politician. Peng!, for example, created a website with a name that resembles the German army's recruitment website and warns »recruits« about everything military life entails. There is also the project »*Frag den Staat*« (»Ask the State«), which, using the freedom of information act, encourages citizens to submit requests for data to the authorities on everything from polluted drinking water to the number of people using urban railways. This information can then be used to base causes on real data, i. e. a protest. I'm sure other countries have many creative ideas as well.

We need them, because it's time to act.

We can't afford to wait any longer. We're the last generation that can still ease the impact of the ecological catastrophe. In the next few years, we have the chance to effect a lot of change. But after that, our scope for action will diminish rapidly. The longer we act within the parameters of the current economic system, the longer we'll remain idle. The longer we continue to allow half-baked political solutions, the harder it will become to avoid overshooting the climate's tipping points. Until the day comes when it's too late.

The political scientist Howard Zinn is well known for developing a new approach to historiography that views the past from different angles; for example, the »discovery« of America is told from the point of view of the Native Americans who spot Columbus's ship, rather than from the perspective of the conquistador. In the 1960s he was involved in the Civil Rights Movement, and in 1970 he was arrested for protesting the Vietnam War.

But instead of appearing in court, he chose to give a speech on civil disobedience at Johns Hopkins University in Baltimore:

»As soon as you say the topic is civil disobedience, you are saying our *problem* is civil disobedience. That is *not* our problem ... Our problem is civil *obedience*. Our problem is the numbers of people all over the world who have obeyed the dictates of the leaders of their government and have gone to war, and millions have been killed because of this obedience ... Our problem is that people are obedient all over the world, in the face of poverty and starvation and stupidity, and war and cruelty. Our problem is that people are obedient while the jails are full of petty thieves, and all the while the grand thieves are running the country. That's our problem.«

Some people believe that civil disobedience is a problem because it causes unrest and disrupts order.

But right now, our order is based on falsehood and destruction. This order *must* be disrupted, because otherwise, people die.

Because otherwise, we allow the system, driven by its belief in infinite growth, to rob us of something profoundly valuable and irretrievable.

Because it won't stop voluntarily.

And because we can't tolerate the system continuing to steal, lie, and oppress the majority under the guise of defending order.

But we have to act, instead of continuing to wait for the current rulers to give us our rights and our future, if only we continue to please them. The problem is civil obedience, not civil disobedience.

No more hoping. The time to act is now.

Afterword

2021, Northern Norway, just above the Arctic Circle. I'm sitting at the dining table, writing these lines. Next to me I have a cup of steaming tea, my warmly lined overalls are hanging on the coat hook.

From the window I'm looking onto a snow-covered mountain peak in the distance. The sky is overcast. There has been very little snow this winter. And it's not as cold as it should be in the Subarctic.

In addition to working remotely for an Antarctic conservation campaign, I'm temporarily supporting an environmental organisation that is trying to clean Norway's beaches and bays of plastic waste. Most of the rubbish consists of nets from fisheries and fish farms, along with household rubbish that has ended up in the sea. Our small team can easily gather a tonne of plastic per day, which we then take to the harbour of Bolga, where the filled plastic bags, lines, and nets are beginning to pile up.

Despite our efforts, there's one thing that worries me: only ten to fifteen percent of the plastic in the sea ever washes up on the beach and can be collected. The rest breaks down into tiny pieces and remains in the sea or settles on the seabed. The plastic harms marine life, such as invertebrates, fish, and marine mammals: they get entangled, or simply fail to distinguish it from their usual diet and end up dying a miserable death. But plastic is also dangerous for us humans, because we, too, consume it via the food on our plates. So picking up plastic from the beach is important, but only a stopgap measure. Ultimately, plastic must be drastically reduced and replaced by other materials, but this runs counter to the interests of the expanding plastic industry, which is closely tied to the oil and fracking industries.

About two years have passed since the hardcover edition of the book was published. The events of the summer of 2019 created an unprecedented press frenzy that made me a public figure. In the meantime, sea rescue hardly makes the news anymore, and I have returned to my previous work in the polar regions.

The Time To Act Is Now relates how I ended up aboard the *Sea-Watch 3*, and why the situation in the Mediterranean is only part of a much bigger problem.

Unfortunately, the situation hasn't improved since then.

The European border police is as structurally racist as the police authorities in the United States, who are responsible for the murders of George Floyd, Breonna Taylor, Daunte Wright, and hundreds of others.

Legal requirements continue to keep civilian rescuers from leaving port and saving people in distress at sea, regardless of their nationality or ethnicity. Although hundreds of cities across the EU have offered to take in refugees, neither the Mória camp in Greece nor Lipa in Bosnia have been evacuated after the fires that raged there. Instead, the Frontex budget is set to be tripled in the coming years. Systematic pullbacks to Libya by the so-called Libyan Coast Guard, funded by the EU, continue. These pullbacks are only possible due to the aerial reconnaissance data provided by the EU military and Frontex aircraft. The agency's increasing militarisation means that it will soon have its own drones.

Its mandate has long been extended to countries beyond the EU's direct borders. The Africa-Frontex Intelligence Community (AFIC), which collects data on cross-border migration in 26 African countries, was founded in 2010. In 2020, Frontex was involved in several pushbacks carried out by the Greek coast guard on the Greek-Turkish border.

The agency was the target of widespread criticism for failing to investigate human rights violations. Its executive director, Fabrice Leggeri, was summoned by the EU Commission; a Working Group of the EU Parliament wants to clarify the incidents, the European Anti-Corruption Office OLAF is investigating Frontex, and the budget increase for 2021 has been suspended for the time being. Some members of the European Parliament are calling for an independent supervisory body for Frontex, others for Leggeri's resignation.

Together with a broad coalition of civil society groups, I am calling for Frontex to be abolished altogether. We need to provide security for people worldwide, not for borders.

However, in view of the current social, political and ecological conditions, we have to be justifiably concerned about the security of people.

While international politics is currently almost exclusively focused on tackling the COVID-19 pandemic, the climate crisis is worsening every day. Meanwhile, species are going extinct on a massive, but almost unnoticed, scale.

While we may succeed in reducing greenhouse gas emissions and eventually capturing and storing carbon from the atmosphere underground, it is almost impossible to revive extinct species once they have disappeared. But without intact ecosystems, the human species stands no chance of surviving on this planet. We are part of nature's web of life and fundamentally dependent on it.

In Germany, a quarter of all insects and a third of all mammal species are now on the red list. As early as May 2019, the World Biodiversity Council (IPBES) pointed out that ecosystems across the world are in a critical state, and that up to one million species are threatened with extinction by 2050. Habitat destruction, overexploitation of wild populations, climate change, industrial pollution, and invasive species are the main drivers of the accelerating mass extinction of species, according to IPBES. If the countries of the Global North maintain their energy and resource consumption, the collapse of biodiversity is imminent. Therefore, transformative socio-ecological change and a shift away from the paradigm of economic growth are needed, the panel concluded.

It was not the first warning issued by scientists. Governments around the world could have stood up to face the situation long ago.

Time and again, conferences have been held to remedy the situation, often ending with grave resolutions. One of these conferences was the 2010 UN Biodiversity Conference in Nagoya, Aichi, Japan. Unlike the Paris Agreement, however, the Aichi Targets are hardly known. The idea was to have them implemented by 2020. They were meant to ensure the conservation of biodiversity, including ecosystems, species, and genetic diversity.

Specifically, the Aichi Targets sought to cut subsidies harming biodiversity, and to reduce overfishing and the use of pesticides and chemicals. Further goals included halting the extinction of rare species, stopping desertification, and restoring degraded ecosystems. In addition, Indigenous knowledge was to be better integrated into existing, Western-dominated conservation concepts, and ecosystems were to be protected, especially for women, Indigenous communities, and the poor.

But as the United Nations' »Global Biodiversity Outlook« (GBO 5 for short), published in September 2020, states, not a single one of these goals was fully achieved worldwide.

Once again, it became clear that ambitious goals are useless if they are not implemented. To implement them, the leaders of the industrialised nations in particular would have to acknowledge that an intact environment is the foundation of human society and every form of economy. And they would have to match their rhetoric with actions.

Take Germany, for example, my home country, which missed 19 of the 20 targets. Most of us like to pretend that the loss of biodiversity only affects other countries, and many people think of gorillas or polar bears rather than common hamsters or great crested newts when they hear the term »endangered species«. On our own doorstep, the main driver of the problem is agricultural policy, which massively favours industrial farming that still releases too many environmental toxins and fertilisers into the environment.

But there are also examples of problems such as so-called »paper parks« – protected areas that exist only on paper, while enforcement is not implemented – in Germany, and not only »in other parts of the world«, like Romania. In 1988, the European Council adopted the Habitats Directive for the conservation of natural habitats and the protection of wild fauna and flora, and subsequently a Europe-wide network of protected areas called »Natura 2000« was supposed to be established. In Germany, the Habitats Directive is enshrined in the Federal Nature Conservation Act, but it is not being implemented correctly. After five years of infringement proceedings, the EU Commission most recently filed a lawsuit against Germany at the European Court of Justice for failing to set conservation targets for the protected areas, to define measures for achieving them, and to communicate the information to the public.

The extent to which the interests of industrial agriculture prevent effective nature conservation is reflected in the tough negotiations on Germany's Insect Protection Act, which was passed in February 2021. Although it was included in the 2017 coalition agreement, agriculture minister Julia Klöckner blocked the Environment Ministry's bill for months, and it was only thanks to a last-minute intervention by Chancellor Angela Merkel that a compromise was reached. Publicly, both ministries celebrated the piece of legislation – although pesticides will be largely banned in protected areas, the use of glyphosate and other pesticides will initially not be regulated in agriculture. In this sense, the Insect Protection Act is a success – for the agricultural lobby. This influential interest group has been equally successful in undermining the urgently needed ecological and climate-friendly transformation of the European Common Agricultural Policy (CAP) at the EU level. While Germany passes insufficient laws and fails to designate protected areas, especially at sea, intact ecosystems are being destroyed.

In autumn of 2020, I was part of the autonomous occupation of the Dannenröder Forest near Frankfurt, which sought to stop the expansion of a motorway, the A49. This old mixed beech and oak forest had been a showcase project for sustainable forestry since the 1980s. It's located in a protected drinking water reservoir on which half a million people in the Frankfurt region depend for water. Soon, the concrete pillars of the motorway bridge will reach into the groundwater. Next to the »Danni« is a forest called Herrenwald, which is a designated protected area. Nevertheless, it was cleared for the A49, which was planned forty years ago. Allegedly, this motorway is in the »general public interest«, even though no court declares itself competent to examine this allegation.

I spent a few weeks in the camp, and for a while I lived in one of the treehouses 20 metres above the ground. The local citizens' initiative had invited people to occupy the forest after all other avenues of protest had failed. Over 100 treehouses were built within a year. Environmental groups and climate justice activists supported the forest occupation through forest walks, human chains, and bicycle demos.

On 30 September, the day before the clearing of the Dannenröder Forest, the UN Special Summit on Biodiversity took place in New York. Chancellor Merkel announced once again how committed she was to protecting nature in the future, and emphasised how important the issue was to her.

But the next day, despite Covid restrictions, clearing vehicles and hundreds of police officers arrived to begin evicting the activists and fell the first trees in the Herrenwald conservation area. Shortly afterwards, a broad swath had been slashed through the forest – a clear sign of whose interests had prevailed. Every tree that had grown there for centuries was cut down. The police acted ruthlessly at times, even cutting climbers' safety ropes; one person suffered several vertebral fractures from a fall caused by the police. It was pure luck that no one suffered a fatal accident during the eviction, unlike in 2018, when a young video journalist was killed during the Hambacher Forest eviction. All of this happened because the Ministry of the Environment in Hesse – headed by the Green Party – had decided it would rather comply with the motorway contracts signed 40 years ago than with the Paris Climate Agreement and the Aichi biodiversity targets. The Greens' excuse: the responsibility lay with the Federal Ministry of Transport. As is so often the case, no party wants to break out of this crazy system and do what needs to be done. Those who do what is necessary to tackle the ignored ecological crises are sitting up in the trees, not in parliaments.

It all ends very quickly once the harvesters arrive. They grab the tree trunk, the saw screeches, the tree snaps like a stalk. Then the felled tree is pulled through the saw blades like a match, the cracked branches are removed by the fast lateral movement, the tree trunk is cut precisely and efficiently in equal-sized sections. Then on to the next one. In no time, the dense forest is destroyed, and all that is left is an open area, the ground torn up. Birds, rodents, bats, and other animals suddenly find themselves homeless – a single tree this old is home to as many as 300 species. The wheels of the heavy forestry machines compact the soil, killing many living creatures in the ground. The construction of the motorway contaminate the soil even further.

For those who understand the state of nature and the living conditions for our own species, there is no doubt: we must not clear any more forests or build any more motorways. Instead, we have to tackle the mobility transition that has been delayed for so long by the automobile industry. A forest is an ecosystem that develops over decades, even centuries. The Dannenröder Forest existed before the first car was even built. You cannot compensate for destroying an old-growth forest simply by planting a new forest or investing in forest protection elsewhere. Clearly, replacing a 250-year-old tree takes 250 years. A sapling doesn't store the same amount of carbon, nor does it serve as a habitat for all the insect species that depend on old trees. What is more, a forest's complex ecosystem in one location cannot be replaced by a forest in another. Quite apart from that, it also makes no sense for local residents if another forest is planted 50 kilometres away.

The Dannenröder Forest reflects the absurdity of cementing more land, destroying healthy forests, and investing in outdated infrastructure that has become obsolete in the midst of a climate and ecological crisis. Although over a hundred treehouses were cleared and the forest cut down, the protest spawned a wave of further protests aiming to boost the mobility transition and back the climate justice movement – local protests are alive, at least as long as the motorway has not been built.

What happened in the Dannenröder Forest is just one example of how governments around the world are dealing with the current crises. They cut down an intact forest while bark beetles spread quickly in many other parts of the country due to climate induced drought. Such interventions in nature are happening everywhere and they can only be called irresponsible.

In Estonia, large areas of forest have been cut down in protected Natura 2000 sites in order to obtain building material and fuel since 2015 – especially because wood can be burned as biomass in old coal-fired power plants. The UK, in particular, relies on such wood energy, and imports huge quantities of biofuels. Biomass is defined by the EU as climate-neutral and sustainable, but it takes decades for young trees to grow and store carbon. In fact, burning wood emits 1.5 times as much CO_2 as coal. In the United States, biofuels from wood are not considered a sustainable energy source, but in the EU, the interests of the forestry industry have prevailed so far. Cars, planes, and ships will allegedly soon be powered by biofuels, even though it remains unclear where the quantities of biofuels needed will be produced. For some, the logical alternative – to consume less – seems to be harder to imagine than getting rid of a system that destroys our livelihoods.

The longer we continue to destroy the environment, the more difficult it will be to change things for the better later on – in many cases, ecosystems may be lost once and for all. And the more natural habitats we destroy, the more our own chance of survival diminishes.

Nevertheless, political leaders still try to do the absolute minimum to avoid stepping on the toes of companies and enterprises whose main concern is to stick with business as usual. While politicians compromise, the extinction of species and the destruction of biodiversity progresses unimpeded.

The reckless exploitation of people and nature in the

neoliberal economic system is responsible for the pollution of the air we breathe and the water we drink, and for contaminated soils. A poisoned environment weakens people's immune systems. The capitalist system exacerbates social inequality and poverty, because wealth is not distributed evenly, which leads to many who are unable to afford adequate health care. It leads to austerity in healthcare, a sector that is increasingly undergoing privatisation even in rich countries, with employees justifiably complaining about poor working conditions. It is responsible for industrial-scale animal farming, which allows animals to suffer poor living conditions, creates multi-resistant germs, and transmits pathogens. It causes the destruction of natural habitats, which increases the transmission of zoonotic diseases to humans because of more frequent contact between humans and wild animals. And the capitalist system, through globalisation, is also responsible for the rapid spread of germs and viruses across all parts of the world. It is also responsible for the warming of the land masses and oceans through fossil energy production: this leads to more frequent extreme weather situations, rendering entire regions uninhabitable for humans and animals as water becomes scarcer and droughts increase.

How poorly this system prepares us for crisis situations has been obvious since the Covid pandemic began in 2020. Crises make our already unequal societies even more unequal. They hit hardest all those who are exploited by the economic system and live in precarity. Despite the initial talk of solidarity and neighbourhood help, COVID-19 served as a further excuse for the EU to isolate itself and sidestep UN conventions on the Law of the Sea, human rights, and the treatment of refugees. Alongside Italy, the government of Malta also exploited the situation, claiming that their ports were closed due to the pandemic and sea rescue ships were therefore not allowed to enter. Although many people in Portugal or Italy received a residence permit and thus better access to the health system, the humanitarian disaster in camps on Europe's fringes continued to intensify, with those interned having hardly any means to protect themselves against the virus given the abysmal hygiene conditions in the camps. Instead of evacuating the camps, the EU once again chose not to practice solidarity across national borders and social classes. This kind of solidarity is simply not part of the logic in a system where everyone seeks to maximise profits. And although 97 percent of the research funding that went into vaccines like AstraZeneca came from public sources, pharmaceutical companies refuse to release the patents so that vaccines can be produced across the globe and all people can be vaccinated as quickly as possible. However, it's not just a matter of proprietary manufacturing processes; production facilities must also be expanded in order to produce affordable and high quality vaccines for everyone to mitigate the global health crisis.

To address social and environmental crises, we need the transformative change called for by the World Biodiversity Council. Superficial gloss-overs that fail to address the root causes of problems won't help. An ecocide law alone will not bring nature back once it has been destroyed. Amending Article 5 of the Rome Statute to include ecocide, i. e. the large-scale destruction of ecosystems, would make it possible to prosecute people at the International Criminal Court in The Hague for committing these kinds of crimes. Such laws could also be adopted at the national level. No doubt we need such a law, but we need more than that: we need to stop the damage before it's done, to address the cause, not just the symptom.

The biologist E. O. Wilson, for instance, proposes the Half-Earth Project, which would protect half the Earth, but his concept ignores the factors that drive species towards extinction. Wilson calls for the expansion of protected areas, so that humanity would inhabit only one half of the planet while all non-human life on the other half would be protected from humans. In his view, protected areas should be precisely those regions where biodiversity is still particularly high. But these are currently home mainly to Indigenous communities. Although they make up only five percent of the world's population, they protect 80 percent of biodiversity on their land. E. O. Wilson fails to offer up any solutions on how he intends to evict and forcibly relocate these people from their land. He also has little to say about the living conditions on the one half of the planet that would be allocated to us humans. Another problem is that water or air pollution does not respect man-made borders. If a farmer sprays pesticides on his crops and these are carried by the wind into a nearby nature reserve, the insects die there, too. The same goes for marine plastics, as we witness every day here in Northern Norway. Ocean acidification, noise pollution – all this won't stop at the borders of a marine protected area.

More importantly, Wilson's picture of humans as a problem for nature is fundamentally flawed. Human cultures and their environment are closely interwoven. Even 12,000 years ago, humans influenced 75 percent of the earth's surface, so the concept of »wilderness untouched by humans« is nothing more than a myth. The problem is not people invading so-called nature, but the behaviour of some human societies.

Behavioural scientist Jane Goodall and documentary film producer David Attenborough argue in a way similar to Wilson. For decades they have been blaming alleged overpopulation for the suffering of non-human nature instead of focusing on the fact that the very societies they belong to themselves overconsume energy and resources on a massive scale.

There would hardly be any ecological problems if eight billion people only consumed as little as people in Bangladesh. Attenborough and his buddy, the British Prince William, recently invented the »Earthshot Prize«, which is intended to create incentives for technological solutions to ecological crises. But the solution has long been known. It is to distribute wealth and power fairly and democratically – which would mean that rich people would consume less and stop jetting around the earth from gala to gala ostensibly to save it.

If Prince William wanted to do something meaningful, he could strive to return British crown lands to local councils for self-governance, as many local initiatives are calling for. The British Royal Family currently owns about 670,000 hectares of land, of which over 106,000 hectares are agricultural land.

Scotland is said to have the most unequal land ownership in the western world, as a result of the Enclosure Movement in the 18th and 19th century, when the commonly managed land of the Scottish rural population, called the Commons, was gradually privatised and enclosed by the English aristocracy. Many peasants became impoverished and lost their livelihoods; they were forced to seek work in newly industrialised cities and became destitute in working-class districts. Living and working conditions were deplorable, life expectancy was significantly worse than in the countryside, dropping to just 26 years in Liverpool in 1860. At that time, infant mortality in Scotland was 28 per 1,000 in urban areas, compared to 18 in rural areas.

Similar to the fate of the Scottish rural population in the aftermath of the Enclosure Movement is the situation of people who are now forced off their land in the name of conservation, which means they can no longer be subsistence farmers. They were previously independent, living from and with nature and sometimes without any money at all, but as a result of neo-colonial land grabbing, they end up in urban slums where they have to accept low-paid work and risk losing their culture.

Instead of evicting people from their land, it is high time to decolonise nature conservation and address the causes of biodiversity loss, which – according to research by the World Biodiversity Council – are rooted in the behaviour of industrial societies in the Global North. Yet many ecologists seek solutions that may further disadvantage marginalised populations. As ridiculous as Wilson's »Half Earth« idea is, it is dangerous because it is so easy to communicate. It was taken up by the WWF, which initiated the »Global Deal for Nature« and thus wants to place 30 percent of the earth's surface under nature protection by 2030. The »30 %«

target is not scientifically based. It was chosen because the slogan »30 x 30« is easy to sell to political decision-makers.

This idea by a western nature conservation organisation is now actually being discussed in UN bodies, for example at the World Conservation Congress of the IUCN (International Union for Conservation of Nature) in Marseille in September 2021, and is to be adopted at the next UN meeting on the Convention on Biological Diversity (CBD) in China in October 2021. Indigenous groups and local populations are extremely sceptical about this proposal from the Global North, as they have already been forced off their land for nature conservation in the past. Moreover, large conservation organisations, in particular the WWF, have been implicated in human rights violations in protected areas in many countries. According to an independent report published in 2020, the WWF failed to adequately respond to or at least clarify the incidents in over ten countries. This happened only after the incidents became public. Furthermore, the report states that the WWF failed to implement effective participation of Indigenous groups or local communities, and to obtain free, prior and informed consent in the creation of protected areas. This problem is not limited to the WWF, but runs like a thread through the history of protected areas worldwide. Especially in Africa and Asia, neo-colonial conservation continues to this day. Indigenous groups have no say in biodiversity conferences; at best, they participate as advisors, even though the land they live on is at stake.

The current preliminary draft for the upcoming UN Biodiversity Conference (COP 15) in China, which will decide on the post-2020 conservation framework to replace Aichi for the next ten years, contains no reference to recognising the rights of the 400 million people who protect so many biodiversity hotspots to date. Representatives of the International Indigenous Forum for Biodiversity demand that IUCN establish a separate protected area category for Indigenous lands and waters so that Indigenous rights are guaranteed and these lands would count as part of the 30 % target to be achieved. This is a demand that we as a civil society from the Global North must support in solidarity. Already now, in many parts of the world, so-called Indigenous Community Conservation Areas (ICCA) are recognised as nature reserves. The communities call them »territories of life«. They continue to live in the areas and create the local rules independently and autonomously. Effective conservation must guarantee the land rights of people who treat their environment with care, while destructive behaviours and industries must be severely curtailed immediately.

But global industries such as agriculture and mining defend their interests, and many of those who want to protect their land against industries face grave dangers, including threats and even murder. Globally, over 200 people were murdered for demanding environmental protection in 2019, according to a count by the NGO Global Witness. Most of the victims were killed in Colombia, the Philippines and Brazil at the hands of companies, farmers, criminal gangs, paramilitary groups, rebels, and even state actors. Putting industries in their place and standing up for the safety of the people who protect their lands is ultimately – and this is a simple realisation – something that benefits everyone.

To make conservation effective, it needs to be reinvented – to be more equitable, more radical and more social. Cultural diversity and biodiversity are two sides of the same coin, and Indigenous rights are essential for effective conservation. But this alone is not enough. We in the Global North urgently need to restructure our societies to regenerate life, not destroy it. In the Eurocentric worldview, we take it for granted that our societies should be role models for others. Yet we are the ones destroying the basis of life on the planet. So, to implement transformative change, we should learn from the cultures that live more harmoniously with their environment. They can be our signposts, even though we cannot simply copy their way of life, but instead must find our own way to make our society truly regenerative.

If we as humanity want to survive on this planet in the long run, we have to consider all aspects of the multi-layered problem in which biodiversity crisis, climate crisis and social crises are intertwined. We need a systemic change that means moving away from constant economic growth and transforming towards a more equitable, diverse world. There will be no single solution for all cultures. Instead we need a pluriverse of alternatives and a focus on global justice.

In the Global North, we need to fundamentally change our role in nature and to create a society that makes conservation as we know it obsolete by nurturing a system that regenerates nature rather than destroying it. We need to change *ourselves*. As the IPBES Biodiversity Report of 2019 also states, we must discard the concept of the dualism of humans and nature. We need to once again see ourselves as part of the earth's web of life. And we need to give nature its own value and rights.

Sixty years ago, during the Cold War, the Antarctic Treaty was signed, guaranteeing that Antarctica could be explored scientifically in international cooperation, but prohibiting military operations. Thirty years later, an environmental protocol followed, including a ban on the extraction of mineral resources. Currently, the biggest problem facing Antarctica and the Southern Ocean is the climate crisis, but despite the promises of the Paris Agreement, far too little is happening.

So while 29 rich nations, who can afford big science programmes in Antarctica and thus have voting rights, boast about how successfully they are in protecting Antarctica, the same nations, through their massive emissions, are melting the ice sheets, flooding islands and low-lying countries and changing the Antarctic ecosystem forever. We need to come up with a very different treaty today. It should ensure that nations give up their claims to Antarctica forever, and that this ecosystem belongs to itself, that nature has rights and people have a responsibility to protect it from harm.

Change must be driven by civil society, because politicians are stuck in a system trying to solve the symptoms of the problems by reaching minimal compromises. However, one cannot make any compromises with biodiversity and the climate itself.

As a civil society, we need to hold governments accountable to act in everyone's best interest and implement a socio-ecological transformation. Only with long-term commitment and unmistakable protest can we create publicity and make the crises visible. As I explained in the last chapter of this book, there are many ways to get democratically involved in order to be part of this change.

In the future, we must not only work against the policies of doing nothing, but also increasingly against false solutions. These include the net-zero targets, which are supposed to allow the economy to continue polluting the atmosphere for decades. They are relying on large scale, illusory technologies that have not even been invented yet to draw CO2 out of the atmosphere. For this reason, the Indigenous Sami organised against the geoengineering project SCoPEx of Harvard University, which was planned on their land and has since been rejected: it would contribute nothing to the urgently needed reduction of emissions and would only create further environmental risks that are difficult to assess.

We should also be concerned that more and more fossil fuel companies want to compensate for their massive emissions by planting a few trees and jumping on the trendy term »nature-based solutions«. It is just another way for them to maintain their destructive business model and delay emission reductions. Apart from that, not all so-called nature-based climate solutions benefit biodiversity, for example when monoculture plantations are planted.

We need ecosystems to mitigate climate change, but it is possible for good alternatives to be soft-pedalled. Agroecology, for example, is a regenerative farming method that sequesters carbon in soils, improves soil health and reduces industrial fertiliser and pesticide use. Movements such as the international alliance La Via Campesina, in which people from small-scale agriculture, farm labour and fishing join forces with landless and Indigenous peoples, or the Landless Workers' Movement (*Movimento dos Trabalhadores Rurais Sem Terra*) from Brazil, propagate this method, also in order to make farmers independent of industrial agriculture. Recently, however, companies like Nestlé, PepsiCo or Cargill also want to create the illusion of a greener agriculture by using agroecological methods, although they do not intend to change the unjust socioeconomic, political or ecological conditions on which their corporate culture and profits are based.

Carbon offsets are another financial trick, a modern form of indulgences that companies use to make themselves look greener while doing dirty business. In some cases, they even receive support from environmental NGOs. Only a few months ago, a report by Bloomberg revealed that the world's largest environmental NGO, The Nature Conservancy, sold forest protection certificates as compensation to companies such as J. P. Morgan and BlackRock, although the forest areas in question had already been successfully protected for years. It is not a solution to package nature as financial instruments and therefore a part of the capitalist system. Experts have written many books about this. Let me just say that we're not getting anywhere by trying to compensate for the destruction of nature or emissions in one place by offsetting them elsewhere or putting a price tag on so-called ecosystem services and turning a relaxing walk in the woods into an accounting act. Nor is it productive to calculate nature as a form of capital or to grant debt relief to states that implement biosphere protection for their debtors. All of these initiatives can only be wrong, because they are solutions within the same system that created the problems in the first place.

Destructive industries must be transformed as quickly as possible. Global North countries are still emitting massive amounts of greenhouse gases as if there were no problem. Together with workers and trade unions, we must organise a just transition with the clear aim to leave fossil fuels in the ground.

But stopping the destruction is only a first step. The next is to normalise regenerative behaviour as a default of our society and to restore ecosystems in the long term. To achieve this, we need to ensure that nature conservation is part of the climate justice movement. And that every proposal about nature conservation automatically includes the demand for justice, land rights and democratic decision-making.

It may be difficult to imagine how the crucial transformation will happen within a short time frame against all the opposition. But we must not forget that no one benefits from a system that destroys our livelihoods. Instead of asking ourselves what we can achieve alone, we should ask ourselves how we can find allies and organise collectively for structural change. The beginning of this may be fairly small, but we need to keep the big picture in mind, guided by what is necessary and not by what seems possible at the moment. Because by taking action we can change what is possible.

Acknowledgements

I would like to extend a very special thank you to all those involved in civil sea rescue, to the volunteers and staff of the NGO Sea-Watch and, of course, to the crew of Mission 23. Without them, such a rescue operation would not have been possible.

Thanks to Hindou Oumarou Ibrahim for her insightful foreword, and to Lorenz Schramm, Oscar Schaible, Victoria Lange-Brock, and Haidi Sadik for their contributions. Thanks to Nadja Charaby, Eva Mahnke, Nic Zehmke, and Andrea Vetter, and to the other editors for their comments and revisions.

My thanks also to Ilka Heinemann, Margit Ketterle, and Doris Janhsen. Thanks to Katharina Ilgen, Sibylle Dietzel, Kerstin Schuster, Ralf Reuther and to Jan Strümpel for the careful editing of the original German manuscript.

To Tina Damm, for help with translations, as well as to Kathrin Henneberger and Theresa Leisgang. Thanks to Alfio Furnari for clarifying legal details about the donation to borderline-europe, Human Rights without Borders, and also to Matthias Landwehr.

This English edition would not have been possible without the financial support of Rosa-Luxemburg-Stiftung and the engagement and support of Dorit Riethmüller in particular. Also, I would like to thank Claire Wordley for the English translation as well as Linguatransfair and Eva Bacon for editing and Michael Nicklas at pagina for layouting the translation.

Thanks to Anne Weiss, because without her this book would not have been published in such a short time.

Bibliography and websites

Chapters One and Two

Sea-Watch: https://seawatch.org/

borderline-europe, human rights without borders: https://www.border-lineeurope.de/

Missing Migrants Project: https://missingmigrants.iom.int/

Forensic Architecture: https://forensicarchitecture.org/

Forensic Oceanography: https://forensicarchitecture.org/category/ forensicoceanography

BBC programme on ›the left to die boat‹: www.bbc.co.uk/sounds/play/p0101r27;

Declaration of one of the passengers on the ›left to die boat‹: https://www.youtube.com/watch?v=7pVV2FiWEsg

Vosyliūtė, Lina and Carmine Conte, *Crackdown on NGOs and volunteers helping refugees and other migrants,* Research Social Platform on Migration and Asylum RESOMA, 2019

Chapter Three

Maps of migration and climate change: https://environmentalmigration.iom.int/maps

Earth Overshoot Day: https://www.overshoot day.org/

Rupert Read's *Think tank*: https://www.greenhousethinktank.org/

Global Witness report on the deaths of environmental activists: https://www.globalwitness.org/en/

Glossary of regenerative culture: https://medium.com/activate- the-future / a-glossary-of-regenerative-culture-c6107a8a93cd
Ecocide: www.endecocide.org, www.earthlaw.org

Bendell, Jem: *Deep Adaptation: A map for navigating climate tragedy* IFLAS, Occasional Paper, n.º 2, 2018.

Climate Vulnerable Forum, DARA, *2. Climate Vulnerability Monitor. A guide to the cold calculus of a hot planet,* New York, 2012.

Díaz, Sandra; Josef Settele, Eduardo Brondízio, *et al., Report of the Plenary of the Intergovernmental Science Policy Platform on Biodiversity and Ecosystem Services on the work of its seventh session,* IPBES, 2019.

GSI, Anglia Ruskin University, *Food System Shock. The insurance impacts of acute disruption to global food supply,* Lloyds, 2015.

Internal Displacement Monitoring Centre (IDMC), *Global Report on Internal Displacement,* Norwegian Refugee Council, 2019.

Kolbert, Elizabeth, *The Sixth Extinction: An Unnatural History,* New York, Henry Holt and Company, 2014

Motesharrai, Safa; Jorge Rivas y Eugenia Kalnay, *Human and nature dynamics (HANDY): Modeling inequality and use of resources in the collapse or sustainability of societies,* Ecological Economics, vol. 101, 2014.

Read, Rupert, *This civilisation is finished: So what is to be done?, IFLAS,* Occasional Paper, n.º 3, University of Cumbria, 2018.

Rockström, Johan, Planetary boundaries: exploring the safe operating space for humanity, *Ecology and Society,* vol. 14, n.º 2, 2009.

Romberg, Johanna, *Nennt es Wiese, nicht Ressource. Warum unsere Natur nicht nur besseren Schutz braucht, sondern auch eine lebendigere Sprache*, Die Flugbegleiter, 2019, shorturl.at / dhJMP.

UN Human Rights Council, *Climate change and poverty. Report of the Special Rapporteur on extreme poverty and human rights,* 2019.

Wallace-Wells, David, *The Uninhabitable Earth: Life after Warming,* New York, Crown Publishing Group, 2019.

Wray, Britt, *Rise of the Necrofauna: The Science, Ethics, and Risks of De-Extinction,* Vancouver, Greystone Books, 2019.

Chapter Four

List of Exxon think tanks that don't allow the health risks of climate change to be publicised: https://exxonsecrets.org/html/index.php

Lobby Control: www.lobbycontrol.de

Democracy Now!, news program financed with donations https://www.democracynow.org/

Die stille Revolution, film on culture change in the workplace: https://www.diestillerevolution.de/

Websites on the Degrowth economy: https://wellbeing- economy.org/, www.degrowth.info

German website on degrowth: https://konzeptwerk-neue-oekonomie.org/

Examples of rapid changes: https://www.rapidtransition. org/

Challinor, A. J., J. Watson, D. B. Lobell, S. M. Howden, D. R. Smith, and N. Chhetri, *A meta-analysis of crop yield under climate change and adaptation,* Nature Climate Change, 16th March 2014, http://dx.doi.org/10.1038/NCLIMATE2153

Climate Action Network Europe (CAN), *Report – Phase-out 2020: Monitoring Europe's fossil fuel subsidies,* https://www.odi.org/sites/odi.org.uk/files/resourcedocuments/11762.pdf

Consolo, Ashlee and Neville R. Ellis, *Ecological grief as a mental health response to climate change related loss,* Nature Climate Change, 2018.

Consolo, Ashlee and Karen Landman, *Mourning Nature: Hope at the Heart of Ecological Loss and Grief,* Montreal, McGill Queen's University Press, 2017.

D'Alisa, Giacomo, Demaria, Federico and Giorgos Kallis, *Degrowth: A Vocabulary for a new era,* Routledge, 2014.

Dittrich, M., S. Giljum, S. Lutter and C. Polzin, *Green economies around the World? Implications of resource use for development and the environment,* Vienna, 2012.

Evans, Alex, *The Myth Gap: What Happens When Evidence and Arguments Aren't Enough?,* London, Penguin, 2017.

Hartmann, Kathrin, *Die grüne Lüge: Weltrettung als profitables Geschäftsmodell,* Múnich, Blessing, 2018.

Hickel, Jason and Giorgios Kallis, *Is Green Growth Possible?,* New Political Economy, vol. 4, 2019.

Hickel, Jason, *Degrowth: a theory of radical abundance*, Real-World Economics Review, n.º 87, 19th March 2019, 54–68, http://www.paecon.net/PAEReview/issue87/Hickel87.pdf

Hickel, Jason, *The Divide. A Brief Guide to Global Inequality and its Solutions*, London, Windmill Books, 2018.

Jackson, Tim, *Prosperity without Growth: Foundations for the Economy of Tomorrow*, Routledge, 2016.

Klein, Naomi, *This changes everything: Capitalism versus the climate*, New York, Simon & Schuster, 2014.

Klein, Naomi, *The Shock Doctrine. The Rise of Disaster Capitalism*, Toronto, Random House of Canada, 2007.

Kropotkin, Peter, *Mutual Aid: A Factor of Evolution*, 1902.

Lent, Jeremy, *The patterning instinct. A cultural history of humanity's search for meaning*, Amherst, Prometheus Books, 2017.

Lertzman, Renee, *Environmental Melancholia: Psychoanalytic Dimensions of Engagement*, London, Routledge, 2015.

Montbiot, George, *Out of the Wreckage. A new politics for an age of crisis*, New York, Verso, 2017.

Morton, Jane, *Don't mention the emergency?*, Darebin Climate Action Now, 2018.

O'Neill, Daniel; Fanning, Andrew L.; Lamb, William F. and Julia K. Steinberger, *A good life for all within planetary boundaries*, Nature Sustainability, 2018.

Oreskes, Naomi and M. Eric Conway, *Merchants of Doubt: How a Handful of Scientists Obscured the Truth on Issues from Tobacco Smoke to Global Warming*, London, Bloomsbury Press, 2010.

Raworth, Kate, *Doughnut Economics. Seven ways to think like a 21st-century economist*, London, Random House Business, 2017.

Schmelzer, Matthias and Andrea Vetter, *Degrowth / Postwachstum zur Einführung*, Hamburg, Junius, 2019.

Stoknes, Per Espen, *What we think about when we try not to think about global warming*, White River Junction, Chelsea Green Publishing, 2015.

Verhaeghe, Paul and Jane Hedley-Prole, *What about me? The struggle for identity in a market-based society*, Brunswick, Scribe Publications, 2014.

Wijkman, Anders and Johan Rockström, *Bankrupting Nature: Denying Our Planetary Boundaries*, Abingdon, Taylor & Francis, 2012.

Chapter Five

Website of non-violent protests, Mark and Paul Engler: https://waging-nonviolence.org

Natural Climate Solutions and scientific proposals: https://www.naturalclimate.solutions/

CANVAS: https://canvasopedia.org/

Butt, Nathalie; Lambrick, Frances; Menton, Mary and Anna Renwick, *The supply chain of violence*, Nature Sustainability, vol. 2, 2019, https://doi.org/10.1038/s41893-019-0349-4

Chenoweth, E. and M. J. Stephan, *Why civil resistance works: The strategic logic of nonviolent conflict,* New York, Columbia University Press, 2011.

Engler, Mark and Paul Engler, *This is an uprising: How nonviolent revolt is shaping the twenty-first century,* New York, Bold Type Books, 2016.

Griscom, Bronson W.; Adams, Justin; Ellis, Peter W. *et al., Natural Climate Solutions, PNAS,* 31st October 2017.

Hallam, Roger, *Common sense for the 21st century. Only non-violent rebellion can now stop climate breakdown and social collapse,* PDF at www.rogerhallam.com.

Hawken, Paul, *Drawdown: The Most Comprehensive Plan Ever Proposed to Reverse Global Warming* London, Penguin Books, 2017.

Popovic, Srdja, *Blueprint for Revolution: How to Use Rice Pudding, Lego Men, and Other Nonviolent Techniques to Galvanize Communities, Overthrow Dictators, or Simply Change the World,* London, Scribe UK, 2015.

Searchinger, Timothy D.; Wirsenius, Stefan; Beringer, Tim and Patrice Dumas, *Assessing the efficiency of changes in land use for mitigating climate change.* Nature 564, 249–253 (2018). https://doi.org/10.1038/s41586-018-0757-z

Sharp, Gene, *From Dictatorship to Democracy, A Conceptual Framework for Liberation,* Massachusetts, Albert Einstein Institution, 1994.

Sharp, Gene, *198 Methods of nonviolent action,* www.aeinstein.org/nonviolentaction/198-methods-of-nonviolent-action.

Extinction Rebellion, *This Is Not A Drill: An Extinction Rebellion Handbook,* London, Penguin, 2019.

Van Reybrouck, David, *Against Elections: The Case for Democracy,* London, Bodley Head, 2016.

About the authors

Carola Rackete, born in 1988, studied nautical sciences in Elsfleth (Germany) and conservation management in Ormskirk (UK). She visited Antarctica in 8 of the last 10 years while working on polar research vessels for the German polar research institute AWI, the British Antarctic Survey and for Greenpeace. Between 2016 and 2019, she volunteered for sea rescue NGOs in the Central Mediterranean and was arrested as captain of the »Sea-Watch 3« vessel in 2019. Her current activism is focused on justice in nature conservation and climate movements.

Anne Weiss, born in 1974, is an author and environmental activist. One of her latest books published in German is »Generation Weltuntergang. Eine Geschichte des Klimawandels« (Generation World's End. A history of climate change).

Hindou Oumarou Ibrahim, born in 1984, is an environmental activist and geographer. She is the coordinator of Association FemmesPeuples Autochtones du Tchad (AFPAT) and served as the co-director of the pavilion of the World Indigenous Peoples' Initiative and Pavilion at the UN climate conferences in 2015, 2016 and 2017.